SUNLIGHT ON SWEET WATER

BERYL GILROY

SUNLIGHT ON SWEET WATER

PEEPAL TREE

First published in Great Britain in 1994
Reprinted 2007
Peepal Tree Press Ltd
17 King's Avenue
Leeds LS6 1QS
England

Copyright © 1994, 2007 Beryl Gilroy and estate

ISBN 0 94883 64 5
ISBN 13: 9780948833649

All rights reserved
No part of this publication may be
reproduced or transmitted in any form
without permission

 Peepal Tree gratefully acknowledges Arts Council support

CONTENTS

Preface   7

Part One

Boy Watson — Night Visitor   11
Miss Catherine — Giantess   13
Cousin Waddy — Banjo Player   15
Mother S   17
Ochro — The Village Crier   18
Uncle Joe — Storyteller   21
Sister Daniels — Creche Mother   25
Eddie — Singer and Man of Words   28
Miss Porter   29

Part Two

Mama Darlin' — Village Midwife   35
Mother Jackman — Bookseller   37
Mr Cumberbatch — Chief Mourner   39
Mr Apollo — Grave Digger   42
Miss Thom — Sunday Schoolteacher and Choirmistress   44
Snake-Business and Iron   46
Mas Boy and Pan-Bread   49
False Names   51
Mr Dewsbury — Dog Doctor   53
Aunt Jane   57

Part Three

Xmas	63
The Masqueraders	65
The Year — Old and New	67
Creatures of the Night	69
The Mail Car	72
Market Day	74
Easter	77
Harvest	79
Excursion	80
Village Fun	82
Weddings	84
Village Cricket	87
The Circus	89

Part Four

The Brights	95
Neighbours	97
A Feast	100
Earache	103
The Black Bull	105
School	108
Fear	110
Of Time and Things	112
First Stories	114

PREFACE

By no stretch of the imagination could my two children growing up in a London suburb construct images of my childhood in the then British Guiana, my grandparents or their innumerable friends and acquaintances. My husband readily told our children about his life as a child in the twenties, as a young student in the forties, of the war and of our life together as two free and unfettered young people, addicted to the cinema, expresso coffee, libraries and the exotic food shops in Soho.

London after the war was like an enormous bomb-site with huge sores of dereliction. Yet there was, compared to today, a kind of innocence. This was even more so in the Guyana of my childhood. Children did not have open access to the world of adults and childhood had not yet disappeared into the mist of commercialism and the creation of an appetite for trivia and teenager wants and 'needs'. In my husband's Britain and my Guyana, childhood still showed marked characteristics of its own, not yet invaded by those ridiculous ideas of fashion, seen in outsized, malformed footwear, tracksuits and other lodestones of consumerism. In my childhood, whatever I did marked me off as a child, a distinct time of its own through which I grew towards the light or darkness of adulthood.

And yet, though there were similarities between my husband's Britain and my Guyana, for my children Guyana was remote and strange in a way that London was not. So, I have tried to recapture times, people and occasions in these sketches, which I am happy to say delighted and informed my children and I hope in turn will do the same for my grandchildren and their friends.

Beryl Gilroy, July 1990

In loving memory of
Pat Gilroy who gave me
the peace and time to recollect
(1919-1975)

and for my children, my grandchildren
and the thousands of children I have taught.

PART ONE

BOY WATSON, NIGHT VISITOR

No one knew when he would come or where he came from. My grandmother said he came from the far Canje, a plantation region prominent in slave struggles, that he never took a bus and that he walked all the way, just as the slaves did. We would wake up in the morning and find him there, smiling, silent and unobtrusive with his tiny bundle of belongings in a corner. My grandma said he first came to visit her as a young man when she had her first child and now she had over twenty grandchildren. How they came to know him she never said, but my granddad always welcomed him and gave him tobacco to roll what they called a *churoos* (cheroot). He was a small, slight old man with a full head of white hair. I cannot remember the kind of trousers he wore but his jacket was always made of white drill. By the time he reached us, the jacket showed the distance he had come. One of my aunts was particularly kind to him and my grandmother was always beside herself when he appeared. She said he had seen slave-days and worked in the big house as a house boy. Slavery was abolished when he was young, but he stayed on the plantation.

Once he came to us for the 1st of August. Until 1938, the 1st of August was celebrated as Emancipation Day in our village. Dressed in white, the old people went to church to give thanks and afterwards they visited each other and dined together. When Boy Watson ate, he had a little food put into the calabash which he carried in his bundle. He ate sparingly and spoke even less. After he had greeted my grandmother he simply sat down and watched us at play. Then after a day or two we would wake up to find him gone. He never said goodbye, or gave any reason why he had come.

My grandmother said that her mother was about eight years

old when slavery was abolished. Her mother was born around the 1830s to the master of the big house. She married and had four children. Of these, my grandma was the only girl, although after the death of her mother, Ayamina, called Aya for short, her father had other children. She told us that her eldest brother was strong as an ox, had red hair and used to wrestle with alligators to entertain spectators at village soirées. She was always telling us that he had a terrible death. Two of her brothers used to come to visit. Such fine-looking men they were! Unlike Boy Watson, they came in broad daylight. Uncle Napoleon and Uncle Joseph often came and stayed, and it was fun to see them sitting with my grandparents to form a tight group of elderly people. One day, only Uncle Napoleon came. He was a very sick man and had come to be nursed until his death. Since he was family, a room was prepared for him; my granddad helped to look after him and when he died, he was buried with respect and not a word of criticism was ever spoken against him. Some time later Uncle Joseph turned up. He was a more complaining, very demanding man. He occupied the same room, but was sick for very much longer. He, too, was properly buried.

My granddad used to tell my grandma he married her because he was afraid of her brothers. He had come from Dutch Guyana originally, and rather than be too much of an outsider, he changed his name from Cornelius Alexander James Mancow to Cornelius Alexander James. My grandfather was fine and intelligent and generous to a fault. He used to tell us about Boy Watson's life and times. He said that when Boy was a young slave, he had seen his masters kill the ringleaders of a rebellion by burying them in the sand up to their necks and then breaking their necks with cannon balls. Some of them had their heads 'honeyed' – they were covered with honey and exposed to the insects. When people talked about slavery they talked mainly of the punishments, or about the daring of the limbo dancers who escaped beneath the barbed wire fences.

We used to sing, 'Limba, limba limba, let me see you limba, like a rainbow', and Boy Watson would listen and smile. He wore the expression of a man who did not wish to tell of the battles he had fought.

Suddenly he stopped coming. My grandma was sure that he

had died. 'How do you know?' I asked her. 'I just know,' she said sadly, 'I just know.'

He never came long enough for us to get to know him. He just came and went like a ghost in the night. I wish that I had asked him the questions which now come to mind.

He was the only living link with the old times who came close to me, although there were old women, far, far older than my grandma, who had seen slavery. There was Tanta, who was brought out to sit in the sun each morning, and Miss Bunchy, and Mrs Mentore and Miss Alice, who had all been slave children and talked about old times. These women dressed in the old style – long calico skirts, close-cut peplummed bodices and headscarves. It was such a wonderful way to dress. It gave dignity to black people and set them apart, It was a potent, eloquent part of their identity.

Boy Watson had an identity designated only by the word 'Boy'. Yet he was a man. He took little from the earth and gave pleasure to his friends by his calm and touching presence. I used to ask my grandmother if he had family but she never said. I don't think she knew.

MISS CATHERINE — GIANTESS

The stories that I read about giants, and those my grandmother told me about Massa Kruman's wife, who made giant waves when she sneezed, grew into reality when Miss Catherine came to visit. Massa Kruman's wife was a giantess who lived in the sea. Miss Catherine lived on land in a house near the sawmill. Everyone in the village called her Catherine Two-Batty – Catherine Two-Backsides.

She was over six feet tall with shoulders so strong, they seemed to be made of courida wood. I would stand and gaze at her as she talked to my grandparents. She fascinated me by the sheer strength and physical power which she exuded. My grandmother often talked about when Miss Catherine had been a young woman. Then she was feared by men and willing to take on any boaster from another village in fisticuffs and kick-fighting. 'She used to beat man to do anything,' my grandmother would say. 'Stackin' wood, cuttin' cane, or sawin' logs. Fightin', drinkin' or cussin'. Then she'd go straight home and make a baby. They was none to stop her.'

She had children: two girls and a boy. The boy was the village dunce and we made his life a misery. When we saw him we yelled:

>Jon roast corn fall
>in the pon'
>When he come out, he one han' gone.

or

>Jon Jon duncify
>Take mosquito fo' butterfly.

One day Miss Catherine's eldest daughter died. I shall never forget my surprise at seeing her cry. I thought somehow that her strength had made everything inside her solid, even her blood and her tears. She walked in the funeral cortege dressed in the old style – long flowing skirt, short fitted bodice and stiffly starched headscarf, but even her full skirt could not conceal the tumult of her backsides. Like two massive animals trapped in a roomy bag, they struggled to get out. Even when she ambled along with heavy loads on her head, my cousins would walk behind her and say rude rhymes under their breath as she shook, bumped, knotted and unknotted the great mass of flesh that was her tail.

She walked tall and straight, and I thought that she belonged to some ancient African tribe, of massive build and untested physical strength. Her feet were like boats. I don't believe she had ever worn shoes – or could get any to fit her. She always wore alpargatas.

For a long time no one saw her and then the village bell tolled for her. She had died.

We walked to the funeral, my gran and me. People had congregated under a high house, and there she was, lying in her coffin, covered with flowers. Her shroud was lace-trimmed and being white it emphasised the colours of the flowers. I was shocked to see her. It was the first time I had seen that great agitated body free of motion. And then I noticed the width of the coffin. All she needed to accommodate her was a single board. It was hard to recall that once she strode around – bold, powerful and worthy of regard. I went home that day and practised lying in as little space as possible. All the space one needs is the width of a single board. Miss Catherine had proved it to me.

COUSIN WADDY — BANJO PLAYER

People always came to our home to make music. My aunts and uncles were keen musicians. They were all very fine singers and used to do their share at the concerts given by our church. They made great play of their voices, and took care of them by drinking honey and glycerin by the bottle. My grandfather encouraged us to have a comb and paper orchestra and he sometimes played a big triangle in our band. We were encouraged to dance and sometimes had to do so for the amusement of the adults. We enjoyed all this immensely and everyone strove to be the best dancer in the house.

Sometimes, a relation of ours called in and played a harp. And very mysterious that was to us. His brother played the clarinet, but the best music, I thought, was made by the men who played folk tunes on pawpaw stem and bamboo flutes. There were also the saxophonists and jazz-band players who sometimes came up from the town to play for functions. Those were special events to which whole families went. But the most wonderful evenings of my life were when our Cousin Waddy came with his banjo. No one told us that he was going to come. His visits just happened and as he strode in, excitement and expectation would grab everyone by the throat. He had great powerful hands and long nimble fingers and he played his banjo with verve and finesse. The plectrum would whizz and shimmer and then disappear into the rhythm of the tune. I would sit beside him, entranced by the cleverness and clarity of the music he made. From a man who exuded such strength and courage in his playing, one would have expected a full-blown, booming voice, but instead, he was a gentle, melodious singer, whose voice beckoned us to join in.

I remember so well one night he came. I must have been seven or eight, and we had reaped a bountiful harvest of corn, and my grandfather had made a coal fire for us to roast some out in the open. It was a soft, gentle, shadowy night with the moonlight shining in splodges onto the ground and through the trees. In the distance, soughing breezes blew, gently ruffling the edges of the river, while its surface glinted in the distance. The river, the clouds, the voices in the night, and the fire binding us together with its light must have had something primeval about them, and I was conscious for the first time in my life of that tangible and all-embracing feeling that I suppose is called happiness. I sat in between my grandfather, sharing cobs of freshly roasted corn with him, certain of his love and care, and my grandmother, who saw me as a special child and understood, more than anybody I have ever met, the meaning of freedom. I enjoyed the singing of the work songs, the folk songs, the songs about love and family, the songs that warned or told bitter, vengeful tales. I listened to the spirituals, those I knew and those I had never heard. My grandmother and my aunts served the cake and ginger beer that they forever made. They talked of times long gone, of slavery, and what it meant to those who experienced it, of injustices of all sorts, of exploitation, and of families who had been shattered by time. What a flow of history that evening was! Their speeches were interspersed with proverbs and other sayings from their forebears. I noted their regard for experience, which they all said no one could buy except from the market of life.

Waddy played and sang some more, and then they talked again of duppies and bacoos, of old higes and jumbles and Moonshine Lady and Bongotoughy and of the dead who sometimes came back. After another set of singing and ring-dancing, we would watch sadly as the banjo was put back in its little black case, and Cousin Waddy would stand straight and tall, and bid us all good night. There would be songs in my head and the good feelings that had been growing all through the evening would wrap themselves around me like a beautiful family-made quilt and I would go to bed, grateful that my grandparents were two such wise and wonderful people, and that God had given our cousin such nimble, music-making hands.

MOTHER S

People in my village talked openly about death. Unexpected or otherwise, violent or otherwise, biding its time, death stalked the living. One was born, lived for a God-given time, and then one's death, or dying-day dawned. The details of all the deaths in our village were kept in the head of an old lady we all knew as Mother S. Considering the nature of the topic on which she was the expert, it was surprising how moist and pleasant she remained, with her round face and small, prim frame. Her extensive knowledge of the nature of illnesses and the mysterious processes of death held us all in awe. It made her a friend of the local doctor too. He prolonged his visits to the sick if Mother S was present and together, in exclusive conversations, they would give their medical vocabulary an airing. My grandmother often looked bewildered as they spoke, but recovered rapidly enough to warn Mother S that those big words would one day choke her. I remember the day Mother S told my cousin, who had a wart, that he had a papilloma. He was in a dreadful state until our grandmother said, reassuringly, 'Purpleoma, or no purpleoma, I will tie it with some horse hair to choke it. That will make it right. It will drop off in one day or two.' And it did, in two days.

Whenever there was sickness, Mother S turned up to give a helping hand. She offered to nurse the dying, cool a fevered brow, mix and apply, find out about the case from the doctor, reassure the living and pray for the dying.

She was a woman I avoided, since she knew so much about the end of one's time on earth. Cloth bag hanging over her arm, her small-brimmed, black hat centred atop neat coils of hair, she appeared at the sick-house at dusk. Her small, black-stockinged feet brought her, with her soft, round face, impervious to slights or insults, to offer support. She knew those who had run out to greet 'Mr Death', those who had screamed and backed away, and those who had cocked a snook at him. She knew that much at the end of life should remain unspoken, and so her gestures were reassuring and consolatory. The respect she won was buried in her involvement with the macabre, the incomprehensible and the inevitable. To the village children she was a 'white witch' – a woman who could do evil if she felt like it. The magic was in her ability to resuscitate and restore. She could get grieving people to eat, and even to smile. She could rekindle the will to live in the dying, but when she had to confront death, she did so unflinchingly, even if he came with torment and terror.

One day I suddenly lost my fear of Mother S. Her son came home, and I found out that he was a pharmacist. She had, for years, been repeating what she had learned from him. She was not special after all. I made a drawing of her with my crayons; I dressed her in red and green instead of the sooty black with which I frequently coloured her. I drew an upward smile on her face and stopped dreaming of Mother S getting corpses ready for burial. She did not know as much about curing illness as my grandmother! And that was good. I was glad that my grandma used special techniques in her cures rather than special language.

OCHRO — THE VILLAGE CRIER

My grandmother used to take me at night to the school hall to see magic lantern shows. Often, I must have been the only child there, although I can recall occasions when my Cousin Nelly was there too, with our great Aunty Tutsi. I would curl up in my grandma's arms and fall asleep halfway through the shows. One night everyone had to dash out of the school hall because some celluloid frames started to burn and then to blaze. After that, the magic lantern shows never came back. Later, a cinema appeared in our village. I can't remember it being built but I can remember my cousins going to matinee shows and then coming back to tell me about it. I clearly remember the first time I was taken to the cinema by my grandparents. It was to see the Passion play – a film about the Crucifixion. I remember my grandma crying at some of the scenes – especially at what she called the 'Scourging'. She subsequently took me to see other films, like 'The Robe', 'Ben Hur' and 'Imitation of Life', a film which was talked about in our village for many months. The half-white children had a hard time. They were accused of Judasing their black half.

Apart from playing loud music before the films started, the cinema owners used to employ the village crier to advertise the shows. He was a little old man with a cap of downy white hair which emphasised the black colour of his face. He moved in an agile, sharp-pointed way and because of his small size, he was nicknamed 'Ochro', after the small, pod-like vegetable commonly grown in the kitchen gardens round the village.

A few hours before the films were shown he would saunter down the road furiously ringing a large raucous bell. The children would come running to the roadside at the sound of his bell and he would order us to stand and listen to what he had to say.

'Showing tonight at the Palladium Theatre, de best film in de worl'. Featuring Clark Gibble and Vivien Leigh.' He was always careful to name the stars and then, after some more ringing, he would distribute a few picture cards to us and them ask us in a serious, probing way:

'You mudda got money? You fadda got money? If dem no got money, deh mus' borra some. If dem can' borra, deh mus beg some. If dem can' beg, dem mus' tief some. Children, go home and tell dem. Tell dem to dress up demself an' come to de Palladium Theatre tonight at 8 o'clock sharp – beg, borra or tief.' Then he would ring his deafening, lunatic bell and go on his way.

He always smelt of rum and one day he was very drunk indeed. To make matters worse, a new chemist had just come to our village to open a drug store. He had not bothered to learn our ways and started shouting to Ochro to stop the noise he was making and to move his 'ugly self' from outside his shop. He behaved like a white overseer. He had never ever admitted to himself that he, too, was a black man, like all the other black men in our village. He used white-people words too, like 'stupid' and 'niggerish' and 'drunken'. He was twice Ochro's size, but boy, how busy he was using words! Ochro got vexed and suddenly clambered up the chemist's fat, well-fed, drill-suited body as if it was a tree and butted him in the mouth. It was such a funny sight that all the people watching burst a laugh. The poor man was so surprised at the taste of his own blood that he let out a stream of cuss words. Everyone was astonished that a man so educated, who had passed his chemist and druggist exams, knew such common-class words. My grandma told the story time and again, acting all the parts in the telling. When the constable came to investigate we were all sent away because 'big people were talking', i.e. telling lies. We later heard that the chemist had fallen over and hit his face on the ground. As it turned out, he was a cruel man, and nobody bothered to correct the lie.

We noticed that he had a boy living with him, and everynight, regular as Sunday-soup, we would hear the boy crying and begging for mercy while Mr Joseph, the chemist, lashed away at him for the least little act of omission in his countless duties. We felt glad that we had nothing to do with Mr Joseph. Imagine everyone's surprise when my grandmother received a letter from a half-sister of hers, who lived in another part of the country, saying that her son was living with a chemist in our part. The man had promised to look after the boy as if he was his own. Her husband had died and she felt that the boy should live with a fatherly kind of man. Evidently this chemist had pretended to be such a man and she had been taken in by his promises.

The boy was about twelve years old with a strong, intelligent, mouthy face. He was broad-shouldered and big for his age. Mr Joseph worked him like a donkey, and the whole village knew that he was one of those children who had been given into another family because of some insufficiency within his own. It was a kind of slavery really, but people called it by different names. My grandmother was shocked. To think that a child who was constantly mistreated in front of village eyes was a relation! There was a big discussion. As usual my grandfather agreed with every word my grandmother said. But even as they talked, the wailing and the lashings started up as if on cue. It was too much for my grandmother. Before anyone could stop her, she was through the door and into the shop. She snatched the supple-jack away from Mr Joseph, threatened him with it and bade the boy follow her. She dared the stunned maltreater of children to come within ten feet of her door, and straightaway she wrote telling his mother about the cruelties her son had endured. Ochro did his bit to spread the word and soon no one went into Mr Joseph's shop. They walked the extra distance to Bovells to make their purchases. We woke up one morning to find the shop closed for good and Mr Joseph gone. No one had a good word to say about him. The village never gave him a chance to do worse.

UNCLE JOE — STORY TELLER

When I think of Uncle Joe, one word comes to mind. Kindness. He was kind to all men and all things. He probably thought that God put the beach and all its creatures in his charge. He would show us the barnacles that attached themselves to the bottom of the boat and impressed upon us the necessity for caulking and pitching. 'De roarin' sea can be a frien', but a mortal foe in the time a trouble!' he would say in a voice that seemed to be squeezed out from somewhere deep inside him. He was certainly an authority on the sea.

When he brought his crop of cocoa beans from up-river there would be dozens of children busy 'helaping' him to make ready for market day. His orders to us were always prefaced with the words 'You lil picknie', or 'You big one dem'. And then he would tell us what to do. We worked willingly out of anticipation of the story he was bound to tell us when time was in hand. He broke open the cocoa pods with a sharp cutlass, and we scooped out the beans and spread them on the hessian bags to dry. 'No put mo,' he would warn us, 'Le' sun get betwin.' When the beans were dry we held the bags open for him to bag them up. Then we rolled up the hessian pieces and carried them to the boat.

He was a man of average height, middle-aged, with a growth of pepper-and-salt beard that concealed his features. He had never married and lived with his sister, a sour, hard-faced woman who redeemed herself from our total dislike by making the most mouthwatering coconut sugarcakes. Even when she spooned the crumbs into our hands she never smiled. I used to follow her to her house and ask her about Joey, her pet canary. Uncle Joe also had a brother who was a tanner. His tannery gave our village one of its smells and when Mr Paul died and his tannery was pulled down, a part of our village died also.

Uncle Joe sometimes tended a vegetable garden behind his house, but most of the time he could be found beachcombing. When he found something out of the ordinary, he blew his conch and people would come running out of their houses in answer to it. People said he had found treasure that the slave owners had hidden when trouble came upon them from across the water, but Uncle Joe always said, 'Treasure, I don' know dat word.' Twice that I can remember, he blew his conch. Once was the day a dead whale was washed up. I shall never forget the sight of it. It was a great mountain of a carcass, black and sand-stained.

Standing on one side of it, I could barely see over it, or be seen from the other side, as people had tried to pile rubbish over it. The smell was unbearable. No one knew what to do with that mountain of rotting flesh. The police, the commissary and the sanitary inspector came, gingerly walked round, tied handkerchiefs across their faces and then went away again. Flies flocked to the feast and the smell.

Scavenger fish, called 'four eyes' because they had two pairs of eyes set one above the other, came too. These were extraordinary fish, my grandpa said. They used two of their eyes for finding food and the other pair for spotting their enemies. Vultures, crabs, sea worms of various kinds, even sea gulls came to it. It was a large feast and they made slow work of it. The smell spread like a plague. The people who lived nearest to it began to vomit. A new sickness was coming they said. So the authorities from the town were summoned. Then Uncle Joe and some other men took matters into their own hands and decided that the carcass must be buried. They began to dig. The masks they wore stuck to their faces with the sweat that poured out of them. They dug the biggest hole I had ever seen. Then they hooked ropes into the enormous bones, and pulled the whale along the sand towards the hole. When at last they reached the hole, it could not really contain the whale. After a lot of coming and going and shouting at the children to 'Keep 'way', a dredger from the estate came racing along the sand. In next to no time an enormous hole appeared and in went the carcass. We marked the spot with a cross made of stones and shells and someone wrote 'Whale-Child of God' on the sand. The sea came up overnight and in the morning everything was gone.

Another afternoon, the fishermen brought in a manatee. We call it a water-cow. Some people think of the flesh as a great delicacy. When the sound of the conch was heard, people ran out of their houses. It was raining, and they covered themselves with bits of tarpaulin, hessian bags and banana leaves. We children simply donned calabashes and ran out into the pouring rain. When we got to the beach, the fishermen had already loaded the dead manatee into a cart, and were cutting it up according to buyer's choice. They made way for my grandma, whom I had followed. They expected her to buy a lot, since she had a large family. The flesh of the manatee looked like pork, but the blood ran bright red. The fat seemed opaque, and the whole thing smelt of the sea. My grandma took a large piece home, cooked it in cassereep and served it with rice and callalou. I didn't enjoy the manatee flesh. Just as soon as I could, I gave up eating meat altogether.

Uncle Joe called at our house to pick some pawpaw leaves to tenderise his manatee meat. As usual, we helped to bruise the leaves and, as it was a special day, he told us one of his stories. He began, 'Look ya, picknie, Look ya! You want fe hear de story or nat. Then si' quiat an' listen!'

'Wan day, ah night, time when eberybady ah sleep, James and Jahn go out at watah side een dem boat fe ketch fish. De night so dark dem frighten, but dem put dem net in de boat, tek up de oar and start ah paddle. Pish-pish! Pish-pish! Dem a paddle till dem do out ah sight of house and lan'. Den James seh, "Stap Jahn! Heh is a good place fe t'row out de net. Gie me a han' wid it." Dem pu' down de oar and dem tek de net and t'row it at de watah wid all dem strength. De net fall at de watah, bujum! Ah so de watah a foam an' run. De net sink down to de battam ah de sea where de fish spend dem time feedin' an' growin' big and fat. Aftah de net sink right down, Jahn seh, 'James time fe haul up.' Dem haul up de net. And so dem breat' ah bump and come. Ah so de cord ah burn dem han'. But when dem get de net in ah de boat, hm, dem so su'prise. Dem look eenside. Dem see seaweed. Dem see rotton wood. Dem see rubbis'. Dem see dis. Dem see dat. Dem no see wan single fish. Dem try t'ree more time. Den James seh Jahn, "Fish na ah run tonight. Might as well give up an' go home." Den Jahn seh, "Cas' you eye yandah. Look, sombady ah come!" Ah so de bady walk ah de watah. Foot at de watah top. Foot neveah ah sink down. Dem look again and dem holler out togeddah. "Boy ah Jeses! Ah Jeses ah walk a de watah. Jeses de chile of Gawd."

'Jeses say, "Heh, James and Jahn. How so, me ole spar. Ketch anything yet?" "Massa, dem seh, we toil all night, till now foreday marnin' but de net so empty. We neveah ketch nothin'. Not a single fish a play ah de sea tenight." Jeses listen to dem good. Den he start a laugh. "You sure you try?" Dem shake dem head. Jeses say try agin. "When I say t'row, you t'row in de net." Jeses say t'row. Dem t'row. Jeses seh, "Haul up now!" Dem try fe haul up, but de net so heby... so heby it want fe break dem han'.

'Dem grunt. Dem sweat. Dem grabble, dem groan, and den dem get de net inside a de boat. When dem look inside, dem see all kinda fish. Dem see mullet. Dem see grouper, dem see snapper. Bringle, gillbaker, macherel and snook a flounce about inside ah de net. Sword fish si' down meek an' mile inside ah de net. James and Jahn raise dem eyes to heben and start dere and den to believe in the mercy of Almighty Gawd and thank him for de work of his son Jeses Christ.'

All the while Uncle Joe talked, he acted the story and by the end my comprehension of the details would be total and I would join him this time in the chorus of 'I would make you fishers of men' in a state of bliss.

If we were lucky, we had an encore either of Ruth and Naomi, or of Lazarus and his dog, Moreover. In vain did my Aunt Ella tell Uncle Joe that 'moreover' was not the name of the dog, but was Bible talk for 'on top of everything else'. But Uncle Joe persisted in his understanding of the text and after a time we asked for the story of Lazarus and Moreover the dog who came and licked up Lazarus' sore. Uncle Joe told us the Gospel of St. Mark in Creole, and I remember it to this day. Uncle Joe died suddenly one day. They found him sitting on the sand, his head against his boat – a smile on his face and the wind playing with the fine threads of his beard.

We went to look at his garden. His cockscomb and batchelors' buttons were still growing, but he had gone. I peeped through the manicole walls of his kitchen. Except for the fact that his sister looked sadder, she was much the same. Her son was under heavy manners yet again. Her canaries chirruped noisily, while he knelt on a grater with a flat iron in each hand. 'Sep-sep,' whispered my cousin. But for fear of being caught joking with us he never turned round.

SISTER DANIELS — CRECHE-MOTHER

Sister Daniels was creche-mother to the young plantation children whose parents worked in the canefields from 'day-dawn to dusk'. She was also schoolteacher to the older ones. We used to stand outside the school, a low building without windows. The walls reached a little more than halfway to the corrugated iron roof, and left a sizable gap all the way round for ventilation. Every time we visited our Auntie, who lived on the plantation because of her husband's work, we had to pass by the school. We could hear the children chanting their lessons a mile away. The closer we got, the more distinct the content of the chanting became, and we could join in. Sister Daniels always led the activity while pointing to the blackboard, beating time or calling children to order. All of them, from the time they could talk, joined in the chanting of tables from two to twelve times, and in the spelling of words both familiar and unfamiliar. Cee-ay-tee – kyat; bee-ay-tee – bat; cee-ay-r – kyar; tee-r-ee – tree, etc.

What I loved most was to join in chanting the alphabet. My grandma would walk on while I stopped on the road outside the school, listening to the beat of the whip on the board while Sister Daniels led the chanting, her voice coming in on the ends of the lines.

A B C – all together
D E F – a little louder
G H I – Ah kyant hear you
J K L – Ah mus' hear you

When they got to Y, Z they started to count from one to a hundred. Sometimes they clapped when they counted. The children came from the 'ranges', a terrace of mud-walled huts with corrugated roofs constituting what in those days was openly called the 'Nigger Yard'. At that time the workers in the ranges were mostly Barbadians, but not long after, this importation of labour was stopped by the estate management. They brought men, every Sunday afternoon, from the neighbouring villages instead. The men used the creches to hang their hammocks at night, and were gone by the time the children arrived each morning. The canecutters passed through our village at dusk every Sunday afternoon, packed like sardines standing on their tails, at the end of a journey of up to twenty or thirty miles. They went back to their families on Friday nights in the same way – but with wages in their pockets.

When the plantation children outgrew Sister Daniels' school, they came to the local school; and some of the village children used to attack them. Considering that some were the same age as myself, I knew very little about them. I was always very wary of them and their champion fighters, Duffy and Boyson, and their sister Carnetta. They went to the Adventist church on Saturdays and, if challenged, they took off their clothes and folded them up neatly before they fought. Carnetta always minded the clothes so as to prevent them from getting lost or torn. They were extremely strong fighters.

All the children in our village had set tasks. My cousins sold surplus provisions round the houses, cut grass for the animals or took them to graze, collected and sold eggs, and fetched water from the well. I looked after dozens of turkey poults and chickens, earmarking those that had the pip and couldn't peck properly. I also had to fetch water for dowsing the pigs at midday. It took eight buckets to fill the barrel. It meant eight walks to the pond with my bucket and back again. Leaves were put inside to prevent the water from spilling.

We used to see the children from the 'Nigger Yard' fetching water from the well. Although we had little to do with them, we did not actively despise them. To us, the 'Nigger Yard' was just a place which people like ourselves did not associate with, but on looking back I can see that the systems of race, colour and class were deeply embedded in the naming of the place and our attitudes to its inhabitants.

The voices of those children remain with me, the chanting of their tables, and the yelling of half-understood songs to please their teacher.

>Come show me you' moshan
>Tara rarara
>Come show we you moshan
>For you like-a sugar and she like-a-plum.

or more poignantly

>Lan' and hope and gloree
>Mudder ah defree
>How kyan we exall de
>Shoo was bann ah dee.

Sister Daniels, fat round face alert, fat round arms swaying in time to clash the beat on the blackboard, is with me too. I remember that I bid her 'good morning' whenever I met her. She would peer at me without a drop of recognition and reply, 'Good morning – am, chile'. Come to think of it, she smelt sometimes, as though she had been marinaded overnight in white rum, but that made no difference to me.

EDDIE — SINGER AND MAN OF WORDS

He lived in his own extraordinary world: a world of elegance, education and fantasy that contrasted with his real, workaday life as a painter and decorator. He came to visit my aunts and advised them freely in matters of etiquette, romance and sophistication. He was a slight man with a firm, well-shaped head and features that showed that someone among his progenitors had been 'whitened' or 'washed', as people said in those days. What fascinated me about him were the words he used to insult what he called plebeians or plebs. They all suffered from dementia praecox, or praecox dementia. When he came to visit, he stayed to talk, and often outstayed his welcome. One of my aunts would stealthily turn the broom upside down behind the door, for it was commonly believed that such an act created a sense of unease in a visitor. It did not work with Eddie. He stayed until he was ready to go home, Whenever he came he sang to us: 'Macushula', 'Trees' and 'In a Monastery Garden'. He would clear his throat deliberately, assume a characteristic pose, and start to sing. He sang at weddings, during the signing of the register, and was much sought after for that purpose. At concerts he played the violin but the tune always came out weird and amateurish. People applauded with two fingers. He was a personality in our village. He came from a genteel family which had not survived the wear and tear of time.

He cultivated and studied buffoonery, made anarchic statements intended to shatter dearly held beliefs, and confused his friends with his surrealism. He would argue that the devil was an angel in a didactic, determined, scratchy way, but underneath it all there was a well-read and educated man. I remember his strong voice and his strong features, his deliberate and courtly manners, and the way he kissed the hands of my nubile cousins. Had he the opportunity, he would have been a scholarly man doing some distinguished work with confidence and flair.

He used to go away for long periods and then turn up full of stories about his exploits. My aunts would say that his imagination took him round the world, and I would spend hours wondering just how he did it. I often conjured up a picture of him riding a camel across land and sea, with his imagination bobbing up and down in a carpet bag beside him.

He had been everywhere, done everything and told the best stories of anyone I knew. Time left no age-marks on him. He seemed to have been caught in youth's time-warp. Although he lived to a ripe old age, he was young when he died a few years ago.

MISS PORTER

Miss Porter had two irritating qualities. She was both officious and ubiquitous. She had a handicapped son called Cyril who used to follow us out on the sands to play. He tiptoed when he walked, dribbled a great deal, became completely confused without any reason and bawled for 'Mudder'. 'Mudder', dark-faced, round-bodied and young, with eyes which seemed to glow from an everlasting source deep inside her, always came running. She never asked what was the matter but, as I was the only girl and expected to smother him with attention, simply accused me of some diabolical crime against his person. I defended my ground with vigour. 'You lie, I never pinched him.' 'You damn lie, I never kicked him. For a big woman, you too damn lie.' I was copying my grandfather in content and tone. She would then grab me with one hand and Cyril with the other and drag us all the way along the sand to complain to my grandmother. 'She say damn to me.' Sometimes I got hit by my aunt for being 'rude to Miss Porter'. It was as if the adults felt obliged to appease her. I would be quietly catching crabs and she would materialise, and begin to nag, 'Come out a de mud. Dey didn' send you dere. Go on home. Dey waitin' for you home where a girlchild should be.'

She was neither kith or kin, and yet here she was trying to control my behaviour.

If I gave her a dirty look, she would threaten to tell my grandmother that 'I look her bad eye.' If I answered back, the charge would be that 'I give her rudeness.' If I ignored her, it would be that 'I turned my backside on her.' One day, she complained about a girl called Girlie. What the charge was no one knew but she succeeded in getting Girlie beaten up by her uncle. We watched her smile at the first blow, nod and then set off home with Cyril. All the children became frightened of her and ran off when they saw her coming. We stopped playing with Cyril, and they often stood alone together on the sands. If she called us, offered us sweets or sugarcake or kite-paper as a bribe to play with Cyril, we still ran off screaming. If she appeared in our midst when we were picking buruburu (a wild berry) or Job's tears (a bead) from the roadside, we ran off squealing that she was trying to bewitch us. She came to see my grandparents and offered to take my cousin and I fishing. We refused to go with her and accused her of wanting to drown us. She gave Girlie a pretty kerchief and some pieces of print for dolls' clothes. Girlie threw them in the pig-trough and tittered nervously when they became engulfed in mush.

My aunt pleaded with groups of us to 'talk to poor Miss Porter' and to play with Cyril. She explained that he was now housebound and wet his trousers again. We countered with the accusation that she was an 'ole hige' and wanted blood from us. When we resisted her, she lied so that we could be punished. My grandmother listened attentively.

'Children,' she said, 'they tell you something sometime. Pity for Cyril blind us to his mother fault.'

Cyril died one day, quietly from a fever and a cold. His mother was demented with grief. She left our village. She was the most meddlesome woman I ever met. She lived in a little house with her son whose daily care did not absorb all her creative energies. The adults in the society saw her as inadequate and substandard because she had produced poor Cyril. *It was all her fault.* No explanatory factors such as birth injury or lack of proper antenatal care ever entered into discussions or consideration. I never saw her with a man. She communicated with other women only by indicating 'fault' in their children. They must feel no better than she felt. Our parents never took her seriously, but we did. We saw her as a woman who tried to persecute us from one day to another, using her tongue as pedantic teachers used red pencils.

I don't think many children went to Cyril's funeral. I certainly cannot remember going. Handicapped or not, we should have all carried a green branch for him, for that was done when children died.

PART TWO

MAMA DARLIN' — VILLAGE MIDWIFE

Mama Darlin' was our village midwife. When I became conscious of her visits she was a dumpy little woman who, carrying a brown medicine bag, often called on my grandmother. She always smelt of chemicals, of hospital cleansing agents. When she came, she and my grandmother would 'su-su' (talk in whispers) for hours. I liked her uniform, a blue cotton dress under a sparkling white apron. From beneath her Panama hat with the ink-coloured band, great soft braids of grey-white hair protruded, and when she came into the house, one or other of us dusted her shoes to rid them of what they had gathered as she walked up the path. While she talked to my grandmother, I played house, cooking mud and sand into some fantastic yet delectable dish for the rag dolls I made. My pots were the coconut shells which we saved for burning when wood was short.

All the children and their parents respected Mama Darlin', and used her name after every yes and every no, as a mark of that respect. She had brought nearly everyone in our village into the world. Her work was mysterious. One would see a messenger running to her house, and out she would come on her bandy legs, hurrying to offer her skill. She answered calls in bateaux and launches, in donkey carts, and even allowed herself a self-conscious seat beside the doctor in his old, battered Ford car. The result would always be the same – a child shrieking its way into the world. For eight of the following nine days, she would tend the baby and its mother and then on the ninth day she would dress it up and bring it out into the light for all the village to admire.

The women would gather round and comment formally upon the baby, the family likeness and sure as Sunday-soup, the colour of its skin. Of course, Mama Darlin', who had seen so many babies in that particular family, would state categorically who the child really resembled. If that person was present, for a moment they would enjoy the status to be had, and the truth of the resemblance would be accepted by the whole village because Mama Darlin' said so. She never strove for attention, or total family acceptance. Both were freely given. We would gather round her at a time that was alive with family feeling, usually morning time, while the sun poured its sparkling goodness over the earth. And in return we would be rewarded by the singing, whistling, and chirruping of nature, and by her loving presence.

The last time I saw Mama Darlin' was the year of the big flood. All of a sudden a flash flood had come raging over the wall we called the 'Pall Off'. It had caught hundreds of people living on that side of the river asleep in their beds, after night-work in the sugar factory, after work in the fields or busy with the household chores. People drowned, livestock perished and whole houses floated away. Vividly, I remember standing on the main street up to my ankles in water, watching Mama Darlin' bobbing about in the sad, sand-coloured waters, amongst her pots and pans, bedding and debris of all kinds. She did not cry or shout as most of the other villagers did. She simply made desperate noises, like a fledgling that had fallen out of its nest. I laughed. All the children laughed and got thumped for doing so.

Men swam towards her and lovingly brought her to dry land. All her possessions had gone. Years of her life were washed away in one afternoon. Her relations took her to another village and I never saw her again.

After the flood subsided, her mysterious black bag was found. It was full of sand. Water had soaked the leather and made the shape grotesque. Pieces of cottonwool and some rusty safety pins were nearby. A peep into the contents made the bag even more mysterious, and for days we played at going round the houses bringing forth babies. I mainly chose to be the baby so that I could shriek and have my grandmother come out to see what was the matter with me.

After Mama Darlin' left, we had a new, young, town nurse who wore a long blue veil over her white cork hat. When she rode her bicycle, the veil trailed in the wind behind her. We referred to her as 'The Nurse'. Unlike Mama Darlin' she never won herself a kinship name, like Cousin, Dada, Sister, Titi, Aunty, or most prestigious of all, Mama.

MOTHER JACKMAN — BOOKSELLER

Every three or four months, the bookseller came to our village carrying what she called a 'portmantle'. It was a battered leather case with two rusty, push-in catches, made further secure by a strip of leather tied round it. She walked as though it was very heavy, and she looked like a squarely overdressed giantess, who had suddenly come to life and set about walking the villages to prove her vitality. Her legs seemed to be strong and certain under the weight of her body and the contents of her suitcase. She raised a lot of dust when she walked unhesitatingly up to our front door. With her stock of Weldon's Ladies Journals, from which my aunts avidly copied styles, and hard-covered novels by Marie Corelli, religious books and love stories by Bertha Clay, she would sit with my grandmother beside the arbour. (The arbour was a raised platform on which sweet-scented herbs, trailing plants and flowers grew.) My grandmother would offer her refreshment in the form of sorrel drink, ginger beer or coconut water.

After drinking, she would open her case and reveal the books. My heart would beat rapidly at the smell of the newness embedded deep inside them and, after being warned to take care, I would be allowed to handle them.

I would rapidly turn the pages and encounter the pictures. There, yet again, among the tightly-packed print would be Lucifer and his angels being thrown out of Heaven; Adam and Eve, fig leaves unruffled, standing in a woebegone state outside the Garden of Eden; and Cain, stick raised high in the air as he flagrantly kills brother Abel. The tower of Babel and Jacob, wrestling for all he was worth with the angel, would all be there.

Questions about these pictures would well up in my mind, but if I interrupted, my grandmother would say, 'Obedience is the first law', and the bookseller would bid me go and play. She was a woman of indefinite age, and her mixed race showed in the brown hair pulled over her ears. She always wore a flat-topped felt hat with a black band, and a khaki two-piece suit. The skirt was long and the jacket had a band stitched all the way round, which marked the place where her waist should have been. The outfit concealed her shape and gave credence to the rumours about the dubiousness of her gender,

We all knew that the bookseller had no husband or children because life had 'done her wrong'. Only the adults in the village seemed to know what unspeakable wrong life had done her, but the children simply repeated what they heard parrot-fashion. My cousin said she knew, and if I gave her my best hairgrip, my handkerchief and my hairslide, she would tell me.

The next time the bookseller came, my cousin was roasting coffee beans in the yard, and the bookseller stopped and said she was overcooking the beans. When she had gone past the arbour and out of earshot, my cousin whispered, 'Maphrodice'. She had a nasty look on her face, and so I knew she meant something nasty, but exactly what I could not say. Rather than confess my ignorance, I tittered in a knowing sort of way. But the term gave me no rest. It was a very perplexing term. Was it an illness, a defect, a disease that I could catch? Was it the ability to bewitch or haunt? It was not in my Little Gem dictionary, or so I thought, since I did not know how to spell such a word.

After some self-mortification, I ventured a question to my grandmother. 'What is "maphrodice"?' I said. At the sound of the word a dark look came over her face. Later, very much later, I was to learn that it was the Creole word for a hermaphrodite, and it was a term hurled at any middle-aged, unattached man or woman. Children called one another that as an insult when there were no adults about, and everyone always laughed.

'That's no word for children,' said my grandmother after a long pause, and then, as if drawing the answer from among a tangle of discretions, she replied, 'You will know soon enough, so I better tell you. The world will never be done with her. It will never get her in the first place.' It took me another five years and nature study lessons on flowers, slugs, and earthworms to really find out what hermaphrodite meant. But since they called the bookseller Miss Jackman and Mother Jackman, I am sure that no one in the village really doubted her gender. She did not have both organs, nor did she choose what gender to be. She was a woman, and dropped dead getting off the bus after one of her visits. There was much sadness at the news. The older folk sat up half the night remembering her, and I took out my favourite book bought off her, and read my favourite pages over again. The book was called 'Barabas'. I must have been seven years old at the time.

I am still eager to find out why I read about Barabas on the cross when I heard of Miss Jackman's death.

MR CUMBERBATCH — CHIEF MOURNER

We grew up going to funerals. I lost my parrot through being taken to a funeral miles away from home. My granddad trimmed its wings before we set out, but we stayed there long enough for them to grow again and my parrot flew away. I can recall the number of times I was made to touch the cold brow of a corpse so that I could get what my grandmother called the feel of death. It was also the final act of parting. The younger children were not allowed to touch. They were lifted from one side of the coffin to the other, across the face of the dead person, to prevent the corpse from 'troubling them' if it ever came back. If a young person died, schoolmates led the cortege, and carried green branches. This was to show that a young life had been cut down in its prime.

We had a self-appointed funeral organiser in our village. He was a tall, haughty, magisterial man, who acted as if he expected to be obeyed. He must have been the tallest man in our village, and had won himself a reputation for reliability, honesty and competence. People looked up to him. Even the most argumentative amongst them, including my grandparents, never contradicted him. Actually, my grandparents were both very fond of him and called him 'Chrissy' and his wife, 'Susan'.

Between them they organised the 'Skeldon Burial Society' and managed all the funds. Prior to the formation of the burial society, poor people and those without relations were sometimes hard-pressed to find money for funerals. Their dead could not get buried until they had solicited donations from door to door. My grandparents and Mr Cumberbatch changed all that. They gave certainty and a sense of belonging to the living, and respectability to the dead by getting people to join the burial society as a kind of death insurance.

The Society had its own banner, which was carried through the village on the anniversary of its formation, and the officials and high members wore beautifully embroidered regalia. No funeral could start without Mr Cumberbatch, and he always came late. People would stand around waiting for him to appear, and when he showed a hum of anticipation would rush through the crowd. Then came an authoritative: 'Now everybody, please take up your positions.' People silently obeyed. The women walked in front if it was a woman who had died, and the men if it was a man. The hymns to be sung en-route would be announced, and the hymn-raisers (those who would start the first note) named. Actually, only one name persistently came up.

Miss Francis Garvin, hymn-raiser extraordinary, worked closely with Mr Cumberbatch, Her knowledge of hymns, ancient and modern, was phenomenal. No house of bereavement was ignored by her, despite the elephantiasis which she had in both legs. No wake could begin without her. She was dedicated to her role and the bereaved were grateful to her. They knew that no verse would be missed, no tune mis-sung and no drunken, raucous harmonies tolerated with her in attendance.

On the day of the funeral, an orderly procession would walk to the churchyard or to the church. No one dared to crack jokes with Mr Cumberbatch in charge of things. People who wanted to contribute to the wake or, in the case of a sudden death, to the welfare of the family, would discreetly give their donations to him. No word of scandal of any sort ever sullied his name. I would certainly have heard the talk within my verbally-free family.

Mr Cumberbatch was generous with his opinions. He thought of himself as a pillar of the church. Tall, straight and dignified, he never once appeared to lose his high principles. My grandparents trusted him, and all of our large household of children behaved with modesty and self-control in his presence. But there was another side to him.

He used to come through our village pushing a little hand-cart most Sundays, just after lunch, before we got dressed for Sunday school. He rang a bell with an earpiercing sound, and I would plead to be allowed to buy a glass of bub (syllabub) or an icestick. He made the bub in his own way. While the saliva flowed from our mouths, he would shave the ice, put it in a deep jug and add the milk, syrup and spices such as nutmeg, mace and cinnamon. Then he would swizzle it into a froth and pour it out for us. It was the most heavenly drink. I never tasted anything to match it. The icestick was just a cylinder of frozen custard on a stick. On Sundays he took on a more benign manner, but not much more. We still had to be circumspect, although he always gave us a little bit of extra bub, because he was so friendly with my grandmother.

From time to time he used to organise subscription 'Old Time' dances to which my aunts and my mother went. They wore formal evening clothes and danced foxtrots, polkas, and square dances. No child was ever allowed to attend. It was the only time my grandmother took notice of a ban on children and left me at home.

Mr Cumberbatch was an extraordinary man, serving the village in a way that was crucial to the lives and times of the inhabitants. He prevented chaos and confusion, and gave a calm reality to a time of grief and vulnerability. He was chief mourner to all.

MR APOLLO — GRAVE DIGGER

He was a squarely-built man, easily provoked and fussy about the graves he dug. He wore khaki shorts and shirt, a cloth cap and always carried a spade. His hands were always stained with clay from one churchyard or another. A large piece of cloth fluttered like a flag from his right-side pocket, and he wiped his hands on it from time to time, His eyes were so deep set that I used to think that they were hidden behind his shaggy eyebrows. Once, he told me that he had been a sailor and knew from which direction all the winds blew. He said he could tell the trade winds by their 'feel', and on that day he said that the winds were blowing from 'Sow sow eas.' He said this after licking his finger, sticking it up in the air and muttering all the points of the compass.

The graves he dug were perfect. He never measured his clients but simply looked them over and went away to dig. He put his whole heart into his solitary work and often sang hymns for the dead while he dug his graves. While people waited at the graveside for the cortege, they often found time to remark upon the symmetry and angles of Mr Apollo's graves.

There was a large tamarind tree in the front of the Scots church graveyard, and we used to pick up ripe tamarind pods that fell when the wind blew and shook the tree. That was how I came to see him measure a grave, using his spade, an axe handle and a brick. I offered him my skipping rope which was a long green vine, but he said that vine could shift, knot and cause dirty work.

I never knew who paid Mr Apollo, but he lived by the koker, in a house attached to the vicarage. There were some good guava trees growing in the vicarage yard and he used to pick them, and share them out to all the children. Because of his association with graves and death, we were afraid of him, but the adults joked with him and told him to bury them six feet deep when they died.

Once, Mr Apollo was sick and there was no one to dig graves to give satisfaction. Coffins got stuck halfway down and people complained. When Mr Apollo got better, he was much nicer to everybody. My grandma said his sickness had taken him to hell. He got sick again and this time they tolled the bell for him prematurely, but he recovered. The next rainy season he got wet in the churchyard and his pneumonia recurred. He died quietly at home in bed, contrary to his wish to end his days in the churchyard.

I don't recall who dug his grave, but Mr Apollo was measured for it. A lot of people went to the funeral to pay their respects. They churched the body and the choir sang for him. When the minister said 'dust to dust' all the children, who stood in front of the adults, were given pieces of earth to throw into the grave, but the coffin stuck and there we were, sods in hand, waiting. They sliced earth from both ends of the grave and the coffin grudgingly slid down, allowing a number of clods of earth to clamour down upon it. The graveyard seemed empty after the old man died. There was a large stone angel in the graveyard. He used to say that it was his friend through all weathers. My cousin said he told a lie. The angel was white and white people were never friends of black people.

Long after Mr Apollo was gone, I used to see him in the churchyard digging graves. He made me accept that people's lives had an end and that the churchyard had a purpose. We used to ask him about ghosts and if he ever saw one. He said he'd never seen a ghost but he *had* seen duppies walking with their lamps on dark nights along the parapet beside the road that joined the villages. He had no family and no wife, but I suppose he had been young and busy about the world once upon a time.

MISS THOM — SUNDAY SCHOOL TEACHER AND CHOIR MISTRESS

Nobody else ever called her anything other than Miss Thom. My grandparents called her Baby Thom. Baby must have been her nickname. Her face belied her nature. She looked hawkish but was benign in nature. She always wore serviceable, sensible, colourless clothes and had thin, skinny legs ending in small, neat feet upon which she put small, neat shoes. Her narrow-brimmed Panama hat was always carefully set upon her head, and when she changed it for a dainty straw hat, that, too, was worn at a precise angle. One of my cousins said that she had fallen from grace only once, when she had her son by a white man, and sure enough she had a mulatto son to prove her diversion from the straight and narrow road. That was the peculiar thing about our village. After a certain time and age, whatever indiscretions anyone committed in youth were forgiven, and the church or any other respectable institution could then be wholeheartedly embraced.

Miss Thom had seized the church with both hands and she took on a serious, saintly manner. Her smiles and praise were sparingly given, and all of us knew what was expected of those who sat in her class on Sunday. She was always doing good deeds, and even when she was helping to bake a wedding cake or make buns for a soirée, she was more serious than anyone else.

Each Sunday afternoon, dressed in our best clothes, we waited for her to appear and we would walk quietly behind her to the church which was her love. She kept all observances, and played the harmonium for some of the services. In her endeavours, she was helped by an elderly, pharisaical man known to old and young as 'Cookson'. During the week he wore his other hat as pan-boiler-in-chief on the nearby plantation. He made us sing unsingable hymns, like 'Christian, Dost Thou Hear Them' and 'The Royal Banners Forward Go'. What was even more terrible was that one had to learn the collect for the day and repeat it without a mistake. If everyone got it right, he would dismiss us early, whatever Miss Thom said, and give us back some of the pennies we had brought for the collection, and we would run out to the bridge and wait for Lun-Kai, the Chinese cake-seller. She was a fat, round-faced woman with gleaming black hair parted in the middle and tightly plaited in two waist-length plaits. She carried her tray on a cloth-pad set on her head. Her tray contained the most mouthwatering Chinese pastries. My favourite was a peanut-filled pastry, and when that was gone, one with sweet blackeye peas. It was such a heavenly experience to buy those cakes and eat them, that I prayed for Sundays to come,

Lun-Kai hardly spoke to us except to say, 'Gie me you maney, heh.' And we would drop the penny into her smooth, pink palm.

Miss Thom would cluck around us, telling us to wipe our faces, or to eat properly. Sometimes, in a fit of guilt at letting us 'spoil Sunday', she would reprimand one of the boys for some long-forgotten misdemeanour, like crushing a grasshopper underfoot, or sticking a thorn through a pair of ladybirds and then watching them fly away.

Miss Thom and Cockson bored me half to despair – and taught me self-restraint, as they screeched and droned their way through the hymns and prayers. But that is not how I really remember them. She, with her shrunken, wrinkled face, which seemed to grow smaller with every passing day, peeking from under the snow-white voile veil that the choristers wore, and he, strutting around in black suit and trilby, are captured in my memory. I remember when each of them died. But they had been going for a long time before that. They had gotten older and walked slower, but I am sure they found the energy to rush past Saint Peter and enter heaven, since they were sure that there was where they truly belonged.

SNAKE-BUSINESS AND IRON

We grew up with creepies and crawlies. Lizards, especially the large fleshy monitors which we called 'salempenters' were feared equally by children and chickens, They used to suddenly lumber into the yard in the heat of the day, their pink tongues flicking menacingly. My grandfather warned us about them, about snakes, and about centipedes and scorpions, especially during the rainy season. None of us had ever been given a 'snake-cut', a kind of vaccination administered by the 'snake-doctor' against the bites of venomous snakes.

There were two snake-doctors in our village: Dickie Douglas and his brother James. They were very dissimilar men. James was tall, long-faced, light-skinned and ruggedly good-looking, while Dickie was slight in build, moon-faced, dark chocolate in colour, friendly and 'talk-making'. He was extremely close to my grandmother, as his tiny, mulatto, bearded wife was related to us by a strand which we expressed by the kinship term 'Sister'. To us she was Sister Jo.

When ever we broke new ground 'a back-dam', Mr Douglas came and topped up my grandfather's snake-cut. They ruthlessly turned us out of the room when snake-business was in progress. But one day I cried excessively, and they let me stay. Mr Douglas made a small cut on my grandfather's arm and packed it with a brown powder. Later I learnt that it was rattlesnake venom. If he was bitten, he would be ill but not die. Another time, he was given venom for 'labari' (or fer-de-lance) snakes. My grandfather used to tell us about the snakes he encountered. One day he killed a coral snake and showed me its lidless eyes sealed in with a film of skin, and demonstrated the stretchiness of its jaws by inserting a good sized 'baby' coconut into the mouth. There were tiny holes running through the coralhead's fangs.

When Mr Douglas came down river, two things happened. He brought us bush-meat aplenty, and he held long, whispering conversations with my grandmother. For days after that, she would be buying extra groceries and putting them carefully in a flour bag. When Mr Douglas went down river again, the flour bag went too. In addition, she would sometimes disappear at night and return with her feet muddy and wet, just as if she had been in the mangrove swamps. It used to quite mystify me, but my granddad appeared not to be in the least bit concerned and sometimes went too.

One day we had visitors – the police sergeant and a town policeman. No, they were not looking for bush-rum, but had my grandparents seen Dickie Douglas or heard of Iron lately? From time to time, there used to be talk of Iron in our house. He was the legendary prizefighter and iron-man who had killed a man with a single blow during an argument over a woman. He had escaped capture and trial for years and lived among the Amerindians and the Djukas – a hunted man. A lot of people helped him when he sneaked into our village at night from the staging post where the river families had left him.

My grandmother lied like a true white Christian. She had not seen the meat, only two 'ignorant' tigers standing in front of her with a big desire to find it and eat it. To her, Iron was Simon. He was a 'nice boy' who was being chased by the 'stupid law'. What did they know of that woman anyway? She was bad. She deserved what she got. Any woman who could not be satisfied with one man should be – well, not deliberately killed, but made to experience something drastic. She offered the men ginger beer and, to show her disregard for them, drank some too. For weeks Mr Douglas did not visit, although his wife did, and held long 'susu' sessions with my grandmother.

Early one Sunday there was great activity on the beach. We dashed out to look. Boatloads of town police with guns, cutlasses, chains and coils of thick rope were going up river. Government money had at last brought results. No more false alarms; this time they knew where Iron was to be found, and they were going to get him. We watched them disappear out of sight – joking and laughing amongst themselves. My grandma could not eat her lunch. She pulled at her clay pipe in short puffs. My grandfather paced the room. Nothing could be done. By three o'clock the men were back.

They had captured Iron! He was roped round neck and waist, a long iron chain hung from each hand, and he was pulled along the sand, leaving deep ruts in it. He was a stocky man in a torn shirt showing enormous biceps. His trousers were tattered. He glowered, grunted and ground his teeth. They were treating him like a beast, and he was answering back in kind. He swore. He kicked. He struggled. All to no purpose. He was a sepia-coloured man, short and strong, with well-set, chiselled features. He had been good-looking once. Crowds of women began to cry at the sight of his pain and degradation. The children joined in. The men hid their eyes. No one protested. They were town police and put their heart into their work. Iron was just a criminal. They dragged him along the sand and out of sight. Next day they took him to the secure prison in the town. I never saw so many chains round one man before. My grandmother wept freely and I felt sorry for her. 'His mother was like a sissy to me,' she sobbed. 'Glad she never see dis day.'

People collected money for his defence and my grandmother went to town for the trial. He was given three years hard labour, breaking rock at the Mazaruni prison, miles away from home. Subsequently, after serving his sentence, old and broken, he returned home. He often sat with Mr Douglas, my grandparents and Sister Joe, recounting the times he had eluded capture by those 'damn-to-hell' police.

He was always kind to children and once gave us a box of candleflies that glowed at night. I took one out and searched for its light, only to find a smudge of what looked like iridescent paint on its underside. Later we let them go, and in the evening we saw one glowing in the dark like a star that had lost its way. 'Tell you what,' I heard Iron say, 'I glad I did hab dis village to come home to. Always a light in dis village for me.'

MAS BOY AND PAN-BREAD

Mas Boy belonged to our village. I don't know if he had any other name. Everyone called him Mas Boy and it was whispered that he was one of my granddad's outside children. I had never seen my grandfather talk to him or show any interest in him. He never came to us. He never behaved like family. My grandmother would not have made any difference in dealing with him. She took in all sorts of people and gave them food and shelter. I often heard her remark that children never chose how they were conceived, but I did not know what she meant by 'conceived'.

To me, Mas Boy was just a silent, uneducated man who lived in our village. He had a mortal enemy. A man who was loud-mouthed, broad-shouldered and had a head shaped like a pan bread, hence his name. He strayed into our village from a place on the east coast of the Demerara river called Plaisance. It was one of the places that retained the name given to it by early French colonisers of Guyana. This man was properly called Philip, but there my knowledge of his name ends. People regarded him in the same way they regarded Mas Boy – strange and ready for argument at the drop of a hat. Pan-Bread was mostly seen rolling on the ground, heaving and cuffing away at any one who took his fancy. Mas Boy resented his bullying and swore to kill him. As luck would have it, one day they met in the door of the rum shop. It was a narrow door. Neither would give way and an argument started. One of the men in the rum shop went outside and picked up a stone. While he shook it in his cupped hand he said, 'Fire, fire, bu'n he han'.' Mas Boy knocked it out and so was by honour bound to strike the first blow in the fight which was sure to follow. They ran down the road fighting. The word spread and everybody came out to watch. Bets were laid as to the tactics each would use. Mas Boy was an accomplished teeth-grinder and knife thrower. Pan-Bread was expert on lassoing his enemies with hooks attached to the ropes. My cousin and I laid bets using our pancakes, fruit and weekend pennies. He bet on Pan-Bread. I bet on Mas Boy. My heart missed a beat every time Pan-Bread hurled his lasso in Mas Boy's direction. When Mas Boy took up his stance to throw a knife some people clapped. The men egged him on. The village needed entertainment. The older women gathered in groups, and said the fight would teach children 'to do bad'. My grandma nodded, lit the clay pipe she always carried, ready-stuffed with tobacco, in the obligatory pocket on her dress, and went indoors.

When she reappeared, she was carrying my Uncle George's air-gun with which he used to go wild-fowling. She aimed at the group of grinning men. 'Part them!' she shouted. 'Stop them! Tell them to stop all the fighting and running and stupidness.' She fired a shot. Everyone started to run. People fell over each other. They ran away from the fight and into their houses. Once again the street was clear. Although some people thought my grandma had done right, we were very cross with her for spoiling the fight. She overheard me saying that I wished she would mind her own business, and gave me a good hiding for being rude. I suppose the men fought each other, but they never did it again in full view of the village.

FALSE NAMES

Many of the children in our village had 'left' names or 'call' names. Their parents believed the 'right' or correct names were private and should be kept from those evil spirits that loitered around the houses.

In addition to 'left' and 'right' names, children, especially in large families, had to deal with nicknames. Jurisdiction over children within a large family was usually confined to a few adults, and this restriction, particularly of the right to punish physically, caused resentment amongst some of the other adults in the family. Not being allowed to hurt with blows, some adults would seek to hurt with words — with 'false' names in particular.

The false name was usually based on a deficit, real or imagined, in physical appearance from European norms. Very dark-skinned children had the prefix black added to their name. One of my cousins became Black-Bee on account of colour, and in association with the insect. In some families there was Thick-Lip, Big-Mouth, Fish-Eye, Flat-Head, Long-Mouth and Ugly-Pattern. Children were driven to distraction by the use of these names. Other children got wind of them and spread them far and wide. I had four uncles. I liked two, was indifferent to one and hated the other, who made our lives a misery with nicknames, more than anyone else in the whole, wide world. When I think of that man, with his grinning, idiotic face and his incapacity to see the feelings of hurt and despair he released in children, I feel happy that he can never again return to cause such pain.

His own children were no exception. They had self-explanatory names like Fish-Eye and Flat-Head. He was insensitive and bigoted and looked, for all his ability to label and decry, like the monkey he was so quick to recognise in others. For some reason he called me 'Chinee Mary'. I would be quietly reading and he would arrive to drive me almost to distraction, 'Chinese Mary' lived by the graveyard. I never had dealings with her. I could not for the life of me understand how and why he linked us. But he did, and it upset me until something hardened to a rock of irreversible hatred of him, deep down inside me.

He, like so many adults, disrespected children and thought of them as playthings, servants, tools or butts. Only within a very few families were children people in their own right. The dark-skinned ones, especially, were in service to the light-skinned, and girls, in general, were domestics, cooking and cleaning for the boys. My cousins were mostly boys and I played with them and climbed all the trees they climbed. I was handy with a popgun and a sling-shot and did not spare anyone outside my family who tried to label me or call me names. If my cousins waited for me to cook for them, they would never eat, and my grandmother would say to them, 'You have two hands, do it yourself; she's not your servant.'

It was hard to be an individual person inside the family. Children in ordinary families had no possessions of their own, except of course their clothes. The 'self' as the core of being could not exist in the family economy of that time. The 'self' is an expensive item and, although the family name is part of the self, the nickname, when it was generously and sensitively given, could be seen in certain families as a beacon on the road to psychological freedom. I hope, though, that the children who suffered from belittling nicknames were subsequently able to lay aside their traumatic effects, in an adulthood free of the self-distortion caused by ignorance.

MR DEWSBURY — DOG DOCTOR

Mr Dewsbury, our village dog doctor, lived at No, 78 in a little house raised on two-foot posts with his twelve dogs. We often went there to collect plants for my grandmother. His dogs would bark at us in a frightening chorus. They seemed to be able to smell us coming long before we raised the dust along the path, but they would fall silent when Mr Dewsbury yelled, 'Shush Bai. Shet mout'.'

He never let us go any further than the top step. With the door wide open he would transact whatever business had brought us, and then bid us leave. His house fascinated me and I never missed a chance to peer inside. The walls were neatly papered with pages from old magazines, and print and pictures were expertly combined, The floor, however, was often littered with bones – some old, bare and eaten down; some whitened by sun and time; others fresh and day-old with fat, dark-green flies fussing in attendance. There was always an overwhelming smell of 'dog', although Mr Dewsbury often bathed his dogs by leading them into the nearby river. It was wonderful to see him walking down the road with his army of dogs at his heels, He was king among them but this association made him an object of scorn to many villagers. His dogs' obedience to his voice, the flick of his finger or a wave of his hand, was something to behold, and children were often threatened with a spell of obedience training with Mr Dewsbury.

As a child I was a free spirit, doing only what my grandparents said and ignoring everyone else. I was supposed to have been born with a caul and hence special and lucky. Even Mr Dewsbury treated me with regard and gave me gifts of fruit which he always polished on his dirty clothes. Some people suspected him of being an 'ole hige' – a creature which could flay itself in the darkness of the night, hide the skin in or under the mortar, and then be free to indulge in blood-sucking of old folk and helpless babies. If, however, the skin was found and salted, then the criminal 'ole hige' would be revealed before God and man. People could prevent these creatures from entering their houses by chalking a cross on the door. It was said that Mr Dewsbury always stood in front of his door to prevent anyone from chalking on it, as that would trap him in his house to die of the lust for babies' blood.

If Mr Dewsbury was an 'ole hige', he never showed it. He walked confidently around our village without any concern for gossip. The village dogs, as if sensing the seething hatred for the family, attacked his dogs from time to time. And when all else failed, Mr Dewsbury would nominate Butch, a strong mongrel and leader of the pack, to take on all comers.

'Si' down!' he would shout to all the other dogs and they would sit, tight as springs and tense as barbed wire, behind him.

'Fight am, Butch! Bite am! Kill am!' would come the order, and the fearless dog would rush to the attack. His teeth bared in anger, his great jaws snapping, his snarls poignant and complex with effort, his supple body lunged at his opponents. Sure enough, the yelps, whimpers and squeals of submission would not be long in coming. Butch would lick his wounds and respond lovingly to his master's voice and to the children who came forward to feed him scraps of bread. Mr Dewsbury did not like Butch being fed by others and would meticulously search the food for pins, broken glass and poison bait, as if anyone would think to harm so fearless a creature. It was said that Butch's food was doctored with marabuntas to make him fierce. Certainly, he was a vicious and determined fighter.

Mr Dewsbury's lived on his own with his dogs. It was said that he had come from Barbados and left his wife on a far plantation so he could follow the road-builders to our village, where he stayed to serve as dog-doctor. He certainly spoke like a Barbadian and used to cook ochro-crab soup and corn-kuku which he sometimes sent with us to my grandmother. I never saw her eat it.

Although he was a dog-doctor, he treated all kinds of animals.

The white people called in Mr Dewsbury when their dogs were at death's door, but the moment the danger was past, he said they forgot his name and dropped the money in the sand when they paid him.

I often thought about Mr Dewsbury, who was getting on in years, and his dogs. What would happen to them if he died? Would the villagers bury the dogs in the same grave? Would they go to heaven or wherever else dead things go? Would they all become angels? After all, Mr Dewsbury went to church. While he prayed, his dogs waited in the churchyard under the pear tree, which stood at the front of the church, and which once a year grew deep, shocking-pink blossom that turned into soft, sweet-fleshed fruit. I was sure that no one would adopt the dogs. There were too many astray in our village. Besides, it was openly said that the dogs smelt 'funny'. The answers to all my questions were soon to come.

One day Mr Dewsbury went on our deceptive sand-coloured river, near the sea mouth, to gather herbs for some cow-medicine. He couldn't save the cows anyway. They had eaten the lethal leaves of the oleander plant, and for that there was no antidote.

The wind rose and roughened the sea. Mr Dewsbury's boat capsized and although he was a strong swimmer, he drowned. The men faced thunder, lightning and rain to look for his body, but he and three of his dogs were nowhere to be found. Another nine swam ashore and lay exhausted on the sand. Neither drenching rain nor whips of lightning could move them. They barked no longer and from time to time, emitted a 'snowl' – a mixture of a weak snarl and a weaker howl. For three days and nights they lay waiting for Mr Dewsbury to come out of the sea. My cousin Sydney and I would leap out of bed and run to the big window of the bedroom overlooking the beach to see if the dogs had gone away, but there they were – a feeble foot shuddering with the effort to deter a determined fly, barely disturbing the sand. The tide came up, stealthily washed over the dogs and scurried away again. They lay there without care or food. The king vulture, his head bald and pink and menacing in the sunlight, his wings outspread, waited with his attendants under an ancient mangrove tree. The dogs ignored the scraps we brought them but the vultures cheekily and unashamedly snapped them up and looked round for more.

Late afternoon, on the third day, they found Mr Dewsbury and laid him on the sand. People came running out of their houses to look, before a bag could be thrown over him. He was swollen to a great size and as grotesque as a gargoyle. I distinctly remember hearing my cousin say he was never going to eat another shrimp as some were stuck to Mr Dewsbury's face. The dogs began to howl. The old people said the dogs could smell his life-smell from underneath the more potent odour of death. They knew their master had gone forever. Far, far into the night the dogs howled. I stood and watched from the window. The night was deep and black. My imagination took over. The stars had become coins, far too many to count, and the duppies and other creatures of the night were getting ready to prowl. The clouds moved away to the ends of the earth and the winds continued their eerie soughing. I sang a hymn for the dogs. I think it was 'Onward Christian Soldiers'. The dogs still howled – only on a much softer, more resigned note. In the distance I could hear the singing at Mr Dewsbury's wake. The sounds of hymns on the wind were clear. Then suddenly the howling of the dogs thinned out. Only one was left. Butch, the strong one, mourning alone for his master. He howled all through the night. Early next day I heard my grandfather say that Mr Wilson, the overseer who lived in the village, would be asked to shoot poor Butch. I shuddered at the thought. Mr Wilson was an enigma. Like all people of mixed blood he was not allowed to live on the plantation among the white-trash overseers. The fact of his coloured blood barred him and his family from white plantation social life. He was a sad, cheated, discontented man, unworthy of a shot at Butch.

The day had risen to a clear, shining tone. Clouds danced on a backdrop of blue. The howling and the singing suddenly stopped. Butch had died and the people at the wake had come of the end of their singing, and were talking about Mr Dewsbury. All his little foibles and failings would be remembered. Good times would be mentioned. All the things he said would be repeated. People would invent stories about him. Then they would drink the final cups of coffee, and final glasses of rum, and go home until the funeral.

Later we went and looked at the emaciated dogs before the men came to bury them. Already the crows had come into their own. Uncle Joe, who was always on the beach, told me that the dogs would see Mr Dewsbury in heaven. Would his face be made better, I asked. Uncle Joe shrugged in answer to my question. 'One thing I know,' he said; 'they will lick his wounds in heaven.'

AUNT JANE

My Aunt Jane was my great aunt on my father's side of the family. She had a massive head of hair. Her face was expressive of a serious, thrifty, housewifely nature. She seemed determined that when her husband, whom we simply called Uncle, thought of a good wife, he should think only of her. They lived in a house on a more 'select' part of the plantation.

Their cottage was one of a number that flanked a canal running parallel to the wide dirt road which went through the estate.

There were always punts laden with bundles of cane on the canal. Every day of the week, cranes droning overhead lifted the canes from the punts and tossed them into crushers below. As one punt emptied, another moved up to take its place. The punts stretched way into the distance, the bundles of dull-gold stalks of cane contrasting with the dull-grey of the warehouses and other buildings beyond.

My Aunt Jane's house was reached by crossing a small bridge over a shallow trench full of thick, muddy water. I used to pause and look down at the tiny creatures wriggling or swimming in the mud and, if she was not at the window, I would, as if to dare myself, just touch the mud with the sole of my right shoe. I would then wipe it vigorously on the grass, run up the dozen or so steps and enter the house.

It was a fussy house, full of precious things – gleaming crystal glass and candelabra bought at plantation sales. She had whatnots and sideboards, Berbice chairs with antimacassars and a Bergere suite on which one had to sit quite still. The tables were covered with intricately crocheted tablecloths. The designs, showing peacocks, elaborate oak-leaves and squirrels with bushy tails, are burnt into my brain. There was a silver tea-service in the dining room. It was placed all by itself on a shelf, so that it could be noticed and commented upon. The bedrooms were a mass of colour. There was a four-poster bed with a frilled canopy and an orange satin bedspread, sent to her by a nephew living in America. What she called her boudoir was crowded with jars and bits and pieces. It was a jumble of things which no one could touch – I remember her jet necklaces, gold beads and bangles, trailing scarves and peculiar hats peeking out from various places.

She grew flowers and cooked and baked and, although she had no children of her own, people whose babies were difficult to wean brought them to Aunt Jane. I remember her quite clearly advising a mother to help the weaning along by putting bitter aloes on her breasts.

She had a kitchen-girl who was about twelve years old, called Leesha, whom she had offered shelter in return for service, food and training. Leesha's home must have been terrible, because she used to ask to be beaten if she did wrong, rather than face being sent back there. Leesha waited upon me and my older cousin Ira, who sometimes visited Aunt Jane for long periods. I visited my Aunt Jane more frequently when Ira was there. She was a miniature of Aunt Jane and her sisters, whom I knew quite well. They were all taken by the fact that I could read and sing and recite difficult poems, which I learnt from books owned by older relations.

Aunt Jane had a fixed routine for her Sunday. Before lunch, she would remind us to chew each mouthful of food thirty-two times because we had thirty-two teeth, After lunch, Ira would settle down to her crocheting and Aunt Jane would change into her bed-gown and her bed-cap, and climb into her large, smooth, mountainous bed for a rest. I would be told to sit on a little stool outside her bedroom door and wait until she got up. I could hear Ira stirring in her room and Leesha stirring in the kitchen. Uncle would come in from work, exchange a few friendly words with me, eat his lunch and go off again. It used to seem like hours before my Aunt Jane would wake up so that we could have tea. The house was very quiet. At home I could go and get whatever I wanted to eat. The only rule was never to waste. At Aunt Jane's you waited to be served and only took one cake at a time.

One day I sat waiting for her to wake up. The smell of the 'Min' cream on the floor was overpowering. I got hungrier and hungrier. Suddenly I heard Aunt Jane giggling in her sleep. I could not believe it. My Aunt Jane, so stern, so full of systems and rigour, was giggling like a schoolgirl in her sleep! My curiosity got the better of me and I clambered onto the bed to take a closer look. I couldn't see her face, so deeply buried was it in her plump, white pillow. I clambered up some more, pulling on the slippery satin bedspread, when it suddenly slithered free, dropping me with an enormous bump to the floor.

Aunt Jane gave a little shriek, and jumped out of the bed. She knocked over a vase of artificial flowers, breaking the pretty vase into splinters. I sat on the floor wrapped in guilt, my crimes rising like smoke about me. I was guilty of clambering over satin, peeking at a sleeping adult, scaring her half to death, causing her to break a precious vase, scattering flowers, causing a disturbance, not knowing my place, and disobedience in a strange house. I could hear Aunt Jane condemning me, My eyes made four with hers but only for a minute. I closed my eyes and waited for the verdict. She did not 'fly up' like a queen bee, as I thought she would. She asked me in a quiet voice why I had climbed up and if something was the matter. I said I was weary of waiting and that I wanted to go home. The tears came in a rush. She was very kind and gave me a big piece of cake. After that I really liked her and going to visit her gave me a great deal of pleasure. She eventually taught me to crochet.

PART THREE

XMAS

'Xmas come but once a year
And everyman must have a share
Only the poor man in the gaol
Mus' drink de sour ginger beer.'

We looked forward to Xmas. It was a busy time for all the Christian families in our village. Some of the religious sects never celebrated Xmas but by the time the day came, it was impossible to set them apart. Xmas was the time of the great spring-clean, buy-in, bake-in, cook-in and drink-in.

The houses were scrubbed and de-cobwebbed from floor to ceiling. The furniture scraped, sandpapered and revarnished. New wallpaper, new blinds, new linoleum – a different pattern for each room would be bought and laid with pride. Debts made for one Xmas would stretch through the months into the next. It was a time for reaffirmation and jollification. It was a time associated with surprise and excess. Paddy plants were planted in bowls indoors and tended with love so that they could, by their growth, greet the infant saviour. Artificial flowers, plain and waxed, were made to decorate and beautify the rooms.

All children were consciously co-operative, running minor and major errands without complaint. Politeness was carried almost to the point of mockery. At night, I took 'Hymns Ancient and Modern' to bed and sang all the Xmas hymns with a little help, now and then, from my grandmother. She baked for days on end. Each grandchild was given a personal Xmas cake. She always iced my name on mine, then she would turn to baking cakes for friends and neighbours and casual callers. After that there would be the baking of loaves of bread. People brought her flour and joyfully collected their loaves.

As Xmas day grew closer, the cooking would start. We helped with preparing and pounding herbs, fetching and carrying condiments, picking rice, and peeling and chopping vegetables. By day-dawn the pigs would be killed and as the day aged, we would find them 'hung' in the kitchen. That made me dislike meat.

My grandmother would make the most wonderful black pudding from the entrails and then distribute the pork to be soused, roasted in garlic, curried, and pepper-potted. My grandmother never roasted her own turkeys. They were for sale to the white folk. They were mean buyers and discarded the ounces: 15 lbs 12 ozs were simply 15 lbs, so my gran stuffed them to the gizzards to 'roundup' the ounces. Sometimes we put a biggish stone under their wings before we weighed them and when a turkey weighed 12 lbs 8 ozs, my gran would readily agree to 12 lbs, after slipping the stone in her pocket.

At long last it would be Xmas Eve, and we would hang up our stockings. I always hung around my gran, so I would lie awake, waiting till she came to bed. Every time one of my aunts came into our bedroom, I pretended to be asleep and overheard them sharing out the toys many a time. They would argue over the books, the sweets, the toys. Some toys, like the gramophone which squeaked 'Who killed Cock Robin', had to be shared. I had several dolls, including a dougla one, which I took for walks with me on Sunday afternoons, but after Xmas all the toys would be put away. They were expected to last the whole year. I also had a teddy bear that scared the other children half to death.

For the adults, Xmas started with midnight mass. Before the mass, the bells would peal and cut into the silence of the night. Our church bell had a solemn, mystical ring and could be heard throughout our village. As I grew older and could assert the myth of Father Xmas, I would be taken to church to enjoy the lights, the ceremony and the singing, and to emerge replete with the feeling of community. Like everyone else I would follow the bands through the village until the new day came surreptitiously into being.

We seemed to accept that people would drink too much of the

rum so freely given, and eat too much of the food through which love and happiness were made flesh. There would be parties and services to attend, and more hymns about the snowy midnight to be sung. All the symbols of Xmas – snow, holly, mistletoe – were outside our daily reality. Snow to us was chipped white crepe paper, or fragments of cottonwool. The holly, the ivy, though we sang about them, brought no pictures to mind, but the activities which we enjoyed, and the fellow-feeling that accompanied them, were part of the context of our lives. They gave Xmas its true meaning.

THE MASQUERADERS

On Boxing Day or on New Years Day, the Masqueraders came round the houses, weather permitting. They came after lunch, which was called 'breakfast' in Guyana. In former days, the slaves had a light 'tea' and started to work in the fields for six hours before the sun got high and too hot. At twelve they stopped for breakfast – their first important meal of the day. It coincided with the overseers' lunch.

The masquerader is dressed in masks to represent real and mythical characters. My favourite character was the Waxy-Nanny, a man wearing a light bamboo-frame skirt which concealed him in its gaudy hangings. Towering above the frame was a caricature of an old grandmother. She was always accompanied by the Long-Lady, a 'long-tall' man dancing on high stilts. They came with their own musicians – a light kettledrum, a boomba, with its thick, firm sound, mouth-organs and bugles. Both Waxy-Nanny and Long-Lady were comical dancers. Waxy-Nanny had a flat cardboard face, okum for hair and ridiculous floppy arms. When they came into the yard, they 'flounced' for a while and then invited the children to 'flounce' with them. The youngest children were always eager to accept and, sure enough, the adults would gather round to egg them on and throw pennies in the direction of the best dancers.

After much hilarious comment and banter, the organiser of the masqueraders would call for silence – indicated by rapid thumping on the boomba. The verse would then be said:

> 'Master and Mistress, I grant you grace
> For I must go to another place
> May gold and silver come through the door
> And scatter all over de master's floor'

If the money was not forthcoming, more verses would be said – often not benign:

> I come in peace, you give me woe
> I ask fo watah, you give me tar
> Bad luck mus' come from near and far.

The masqueraders, after saying such a verse, would never call again.

My grandparents paid up in money, food and drink. They welcomed the masqueraders, appreciated their dancing, and even allowed us to go masquerading among our family. We made our own music, with a comb and paper, a mouth-organ and a tin drum. We collected about twenty old pennies. Large and cold they were. We each got four, counted them over and over again and then recited the twelve long months we would have to wait before Xmas came round again.

The next day – Boxing Day – we visited friends and relations to sample their food and wine made from rice or fruit. It was said that the traditional Xmas cake contained so much liquor one could get drunk by eating it. Xmas cake is called 'black' cake and resembles the best Xmas pudding in texture and taste.

On Boxing Night there would be several kinds of functions to attend.

If either the church, or the Burial Society, or the Negro Progress Convention was involved, all our family would attend, young and old, big or small; no-one was excluded. People accepted going out together with other members of their families. Earlier in the day, wooden trays taken to the venue would be made ready to accommodate the babies. Young children who fell asleep would be made comfortable until it was time to go home.

I used to circle round my cousins going to fancy dress balls and admire their outfits. They went as characters from legend or literature, and often won prizes for their costumes.

The really selective dances were the invitation-only 'Snow-White Balls' at which women dressed in long white organdie gowns danced with eligible young men in dark suits. The music usually came from the towns at great expense.

Darkness falls like a curtain in my village, and soon after dark the rented gas lamps would be lighted and taken to the hall where the ball was to be held. Knots of spectators would watch the guests arrive on shanks' pony; very, very few people owned cars. Most people rode bicycles, but that would have been impossible in a white organdie ball gown.

The spectators would stand in the dark and listen to the music and, after a while, their voices on their way home would reach me in my bed.

On Boxing Night, I prayed to grow up. It was a very difficult thing to do within my family. Everyone was so status conscious they needed children to order around and oppress – especially one of my cousins who thought she was the queen.

THE YEAR — OLD AND NEW

On Old Year's Night (New Year's Eve) most people went to church. At midnight, a man named Moody Allen used to blow a conch to bid strangers leave our village. My granddad said that criminals used to come to our village in the hope of escaping from the law to Dutch Guyana on the other side of the Corentyne River. The villagers sheltered them for one year and then threw them out.

At the watch night service the church was bursting at the seams with the obligatory once-a-year attenders. After the service the younger people followed the bands from house to house until the break of day. People ate peas and rice after the midnight service so that they could be blessed with both health and wealth in the New Year. If the new moon showed on Old Year's Night, we held out pure silver to her for further good luck.

We were all exhausted on New Year's Day. Not only did we wait up to see the Old Year out and the New Year in, but we had that day cleaned the house from top to bottom yet again, taking care to dispose of all broken combs and crockery, dead or dying plants, stale food and tattered clothing. All rubbish in and around the house had to be burnt before Mother New Year came.

She was never as generous as Father Xmas, since the kitty was bare or very nearly bare. So Mother New Year left only a few toffees or half an Xmas apple.

Early on New Year's Day, the Goat Race was held on our local ball-field. Man and goat formed the running team, wore individual colours and, as it was a man's sport, much money was won and lost in the betting. After the goat races, people went to the boat races which were held on the seashore. It was always utterly confusing. The starting line seemed to shift from minute to minute, people got soaking wet and the shouting and the beat of the boomba drums was deafening. It was impossible to tell the winners. As evening wore on, the Indian gatka dancers came to liven up the day. They would come down the road clashing their long, thick sticks and jumping to the rhythm. Agility and timing prevented the dancers from being hurt and kept the sticks clashing and clanging in a strange, weird rhythm. The Chinese jugglers also came. They juggled oranges and pieces of wood, and the fire-eaters and men carrying hessian bags containing broken glass on which they danced, kept us happily mystified. Women of all races sold food and pampered the children, who were allowed more than their share of iceblocks, bub and shave-ice. With a metal ice-shaver, the seller would shave some ice from a block, mould it into a ball and cover it with syrup. It was wonderful stuff.

The greasy pole climbing was the highlight of the afternoon. A ten-foot pole, thickly coated with engine grease, would be horizontally suspended about four feet from the ground. At one end of the pole was a saucepan with money, bottles of rum, bay rum and a cotton neckerchief. The organiser circulated among the crowd with a shak-shak and invited people to enter the climbing competition for a small fee. We would cluster around to see them try, and then applaud the mocking drums and join in the general merriment when they failed.

From time to time, the pole-minder dramatically replaced the grease, but just before people started drifting away with boredom, the champion climber from the next village would appear to challenge our champion. Bets would be laid and the cluster would become a crowd. I would stand breathless as the man shook, slithered and slipped. He would regain his balance just in time to stop a fall and at last he would reach the end of the pole to a mighty shout from the crowd.

People would hug, kiss, stamp and generally go berserk at his win. Money would change hands yet another time, and then we would drift off home.

At the end of the day, I used to look down at the sand literally covered with thousands of footprints. But just to show that I had been there too, had taken part and had completely enjoyed it all, I would retrace my steps and with one foot wipe off some of those unknown thousands, then leave my own clear and definite ones behind.

CREATURES OF THE NIGHT

In books like Grimms' and Anderson's fairy tales, *Aladdin and the Wonderful Lamp,* and *Sinbad the Sailor,* we read about the supernatural and the fantastic. But there was a remoteness about their fantasy. They inhabited the daylight hours, and remained as words upon a page.

When, however, on bead-black nights, the wind howling a duet with whining dogs, we listened to tales of the foul deeds of Massa Kruman, who swallowed massive ships in a single gulp, and of Bongo-toughy, who had a face for every window of the many-windowed vicarage, the fantasy became reality. A reality that was our lives. The older folk came into their own when they dealt with the fantastic. Fact, fiction and imagination huddled under the blanket of the story.

As we walked home from a function of some kind, late on a quiet, moonlit night, I expected to overtake Moon-Gazer, pass through his long, thin, widespread legs, feel him bend over and pick me up, then examine me and put me down again.

On rainy nights we expected a hungry duppy or a long bubby, carrying a glowing cinder in an egg shell, to knock and ask for food and shelter, or a more contentious bacoo to demand a fight using one of his detachable limbs for a weapon. Bacoos, we were told, had such large revolving heads that once they were down they could never get up. The only words they ever spoke were 'No pra-pra', meaning 'no throws'. A surprise attack was impossible because of their rapidly turning heads. A fight with a bacoo was lost before it started.

The jumbies, too, were a perpetual hazard, inhabiting old houses, graveyards and silence. Especially the silence of the mind. Some people were plagued by jumbies and had to be rid of them by obeah men. These came in all shapes and forms and anyone could set themselves up as one. All it took was a glib tongue and the ability to persuade gullible people. There were obeah women too, and they preyed on people who were heartsick, indecisive and anxious.

A noted obeah man in our village was called Bucksie. He played on the fact that he was 'half-buck' (Amerindian) and dwelt on the timelessness and the mysticism of his people.

Before he set up as an obeah nun, we played with his son Randolph, a rangy, long-limbed boy who could climb higher than any monkey. His mother, too, was sociable and kind, and often brought flour for my grandmother to make her bread. They were an ordinary family until the day Randolph broke his shoulder and his arm. He fell off a tree and lay on the ground screaming. When we picked him up, his humerus protruded in a weird way from under his skin. It affected me greatly. I became aware of the vulnerability and hence insecurity of my flesh. I felt deeply distrustful of my flesh, and asked questions about it. What was it made of? How was it held together and what would happen to me if it disappeared?

My grandparents told me not to worry. Some flesh would always remain in place to hold me together. When I insisted that

I wanted to see my insides, they gave me a sideways look and carried on laughing.

The mother and her friends took Randolph to hospital, forty-seven miles away. After that day he and his mother never came back to our village. We never mentioned Randolph. None of the adults mentioned his mother. They had passed on and out of our lives: a boy with a broken shoulder and arm, and a silently weeping mother.

Bucksie lived on his own for a long time, and now that he needed only to earn half a living, sold herbs and fruit from a tray outside his door. His house was a small isolated building in a little clearing of land upon which his few hens ran. His dogs kept it free of mongooses, and his goat grazed peacefully. After a while he started selling other things. People went to buy herbal cures, aphrodisiacs, worm pills, rat poisons and appetite-builders. When he wanted to be funny, he offered 'Sheep eggs for sale'.

He used to tell us how many jumbies he had seen. They looked just like the plantation people. He had done battle with them, and we could see them any night if we walked alone, dressed in black, stayed quiet and were 'certain-sure, of-course-yes,' to be looking for jumbies. He would give out black-eye peas to throw behind us if we ever felt we were being followed by jumbies of any age or size.

The supernatural was very much a part of our lives. We saw Massa Kruman's hand in every drowning and every capsized boat. We heard his anger in every log banging against another in the rushing tide. As for Bongo-toughy, the moment the church service began to bore me, he appeared. He sneaked out of the village and down the road. Then, only when I was looking, he would turn into the graveyard and begin to play hide-and-seek from behind the gravestones.

He would cock snooks at me, and make a hundred other provocative gestures, and sometimes I would nod off with anger until time to go home. There were elves and fairies, gnomes and homunculi, giants, wizards and witches too. But they mostly stayed on the pages that had spawned them. For me the only valid creatures of fantasy were the ones I shared with all the children of my village. They were our own and were as necessary for our identity as the houses we lived in, and the paths we walked each day.

When we chewed cane, we talked of the Cane Men, those wild, bearded creatures who lived among the tall canes, and prowled around the houses to steal crying children from their beds. We walked along the sands searching for the golden combs left behind by absent-minded mermaids. Ole higes and vampire men had their niches too. All these fantastic creatures were invisible yet ever present, surfacing only when we willed them up. They came at night. Daylight robbed them of substance and made them retreat. In the light of day only the things that gave life meaning lay heaped-up around us: grass, trees, flowers, the birds and animals – and people working under the sun.

THE MAIL CAR

We all knew the mail car, a little Ford car, driven by a tall, thin, loose-limbed, laconic man of entrenched reactions called Vivian. It passed our house around half-past seven o'clock each morning and stopped at the Post Office, fifty yards further up the road. The postmen and their apprentices made the mail ready to leave at eight. They placed the mailbags inside the car, then Vivian, along with the four passengers, for which it was always oversubscribed, climbed in and the journey began. The procedure was itemised in Vivian's mind; it was never varied. The mail car stopped at six central post offices along the route. It was a faster and more comfortable means of travelling than the buses. Because the mail was 'government', people respected it. Vivian was not only the driver. He did serious errands for people who could not make the trip to town. He took verbal messages from townspeople to country people from sheer goodness of heart. He spoke only when necessary in a short, clipped manner. He understood all the idiosyncrasies of the mail car and if the engine didn't 'purr like a kyat' he would stop the car and crawl under it. His voice and manner would change, and become amorous and persuasive. The engine would become his 'dou-dou darling' and his 'lover girl'. And as he worked on the car with deep concentration, little silver beads of sweat would trickle down his face, until he got his car going again. Sometimes it needed water and he would scuttle down the parapet to get water from the trench, and lovingly pour it into the radiator.

At Tarlogie, everyone who travelled by mail car encountered Sergeant 'Mark-a-Book'. He was really called Mr. Hughes. He once told me of his visit to 'the country of New York'.

The police station and the post office were adjoining buildings, and 'Mark-a-Book' always came out to pay his respects to the 'Government kyar'. He had an incredible facility in switching between Standard English and Creolese. He spoke apodictically and continually promised to write everything down. 'Me go mark-it-a-book...Yes, mark-it-a-book' was his recurring remark. It became the catchphrase by which he is remembered to this day. He was a statuesque black man, alert and intelligent, and an intense seeker after knowledge. I often wondered if he had another life free of 'marking' when he went home to his family.

When we reached No. 63 Village we were nearly home. It was only another eight miles to go. There were children at that post office and they came out to stare at the travellers and giggle at us. As we passed through the villages, we would see other children holding bundles of grass they had gone out to cut, or wielding long switches behind a drove of cattle, or carrying vegetables or strings of fish. If we stopped in the market, there would be clusters of children selling fruit or tending stalls. In the country, being a good child meant being able to do a share of work in the productive life of the family. Children were not meant to be served but to serve.

Schoolwork, and even homework did not exclude service to the family. Although I made several journeys in the mail car, apart from Mark-a-Book and Vivian, I cannot recall a single adult who rode with me or sat beside me. But children come back to me: running, laughing, sauntering children; some crying wares, calling cattle, or simply staring as the mail car sped past; children who looked weak, strong, pathetic or condemned to a life of perpetual toil; children who spent each day watching the buses go on the monotonous journey into town.

The buses went in relays to the town, the earliest leaving at around three a.m. to catch the market by eight. Luggage, including livestock, was piled on a large rack on the top of the buses, which had names like Oriental Star, Silky Six and The Flying Fish. They stopped outside the houses and hooted for their passengers, who at that time paid three shillings for the journey. Considering the state of the road, the drivers must have had nerves of steel. Day after day they made the journey with patience and with care. Accidents were few but people who disliked the feel of the clammily dawning day, the uncomfortable seats, and the total darkness in which the journey began, took the precaution of booking a seat in the mail car days in advance of the journey.

The mail car was one of the certainties of my life. It ran every day, except on public holidays. Like a little black bug it would disappear into the distance, leaving a cloud of dust to mark its course. Shortly after, the postman would mount his bicycle and deliver the mail from house to house, and the post master would wave to us and then disappear into the bowels of the post office to scribble and shout the day away.

MARKET DAY

Saturday was market day. Well before day-dawn, the rumble of carts bringing produce to market could be heard going past our house. The market was simply a section of the village street set aside for stalls. Very few were raised. The sellers spread bags and pieces of coarse cloth on the roadside, and parcelled out their fruit and vegetables. Those who came early chose the most central spots to spread out their produce. They shouted the virtues of their eggs, their coconuts, their mangoes to the passers-by, while their donkeys stood nonchalantly on the parapets, eating the grass that had been brought to feed them. When the sun became too hot, the vendors and sometimes their children sat in the shade under the carts.

Everything was for sale. Food, such as fish and bread, black pudding, dhall puri mitai and some hard-boiled sweets called bull's eyes. Trinkets, pottery, hairpins and cloth were for sale as well. The market served many purposes. People met their friends, exchanged gossip and exercised choice in the purchases they made. For the rest of the week they would have no option but to buy what was offered each afternoon by the children who sold from door to door. The price depended on availability, and quality did not count.

On market day, vendors came from miles away. Some had been doing the trip for years. Families were well known to one another and stopped to exchange small talk before proceeding with the serious task of buying and selling.

Sometimes I used to accompany my aunt to market and, if I felt like it, help her to carry home the purchases in which I had an interest. I did not like the market because of the heat, the dust and the noise. I was always eager to get back home, because my grandmother would have finished baking the quantities of bread she made each week. The woodman came very early, and we would be expected to stack the wood beside her clay and brick oven. We would then proceed to wash the pans and baking sheets and lay them in the sun to dry. Later we would grease them and she would inspect them for any spots left ungreased. We worked hard to please her. She kept a gubby of yeast in the kitchen and, in less time than it takes to tell, she would be mixing, kneading, leaving the dough to rise and then baking dozens of loaves for her family. If my grandmother was upset about anything, she made bread.

If we helped her well on market day, she would discover that she had some dough left over and allow us to make our own loaves. The only person to share them with us was my grandfather. He always said nothing could kill him, only death.

Later in the evening, he would give us a penny each for pocketpiece. We were allowed to spend it and did not hesitate to do so. I used to spend my penny half a dozen times by eye alone on market day. As I remember it, the penny was always old and grew larger the longer I held it.

Impatiently I would watch for the East Indian vendors to set up their stalls with their flickering 'speak-easies' – little bottles of paraffin with wicks protruding from the stoppers. The dull glow would draw us like metal to a magnet, and we would rush past the Jordanites, who sang as if their throats were elasticated. My cousin would buy his channa, all crisp and peppered, and I my 'funnel', or paper cone full of freshly roasted peanuts. The pleasure with which I shelled each nut can never be imagined, and the fact that this was a weekly ritual never dulled its edge. I would unfold the cone, to watch it become a rectangle of rough brown paper, a flat bed upon which to lay each captive nut before the act of grinding it into a fine, delicious powder. To spread it further over time, I would add a soupçon of sugar, and then take a longing tongue to it. First the edges would change shape, and then patterns would appear in the middle. Slowly I would find myself down to the oily shine of the paper and my pleasure would be so keenly gratified. I would become fully aware of the Jordanites and join in singing 'Oh happy day, when Jesus washed my sins away'. I used to follow some Indian girls to the 'backpond' and watch them beating their clothes, so it was easy to think of sin as a kind of soapy scum and Jesus having a fine old time with a scrubbing board. The Sisters were always in immaculate white headresses and frocks and the Brothers in long, flowing milky-white robes. Even the children copy-catted the adults and sang as if they meant every word. If they were in luck, my grandfather would send us out with a sixpence and they would take it and say 'Tenk e chile'. I never failed to whisper 'children' in such a loud voice that they were bound to hear.

The smell of bread and cake always hung about our house and eventually my granddad would help himself to some. We would all stand quite close to him and he would test our spelling, rewarding us with a bite of cake if we could spell, and a mere taste if we could not. If he ate fruit he would wash it well and then show us how germs and dust caused the water to change colour.

Suddenly it would become dark outside, just as if a thick black curtain had been uncompromisingly pulled down by a capable and mysterious hand. The Jordanites would have vanished just as silently as they had come. There would be no more voices or rumbling carts on the journey home. The street would have gone to bed and, except for the look of exhaustion on my grandmother's face and the debris of the day's activities about the house, another market day would have gone forever.

EASTER

The Chinese, my grandmother said, brought kites to Guyana, and because gum cherries or 'pasey' ripened at Easter time, it was easy for the whole country to make and fly kites then. Later the church latched on to their symbolism, and at Sunday School they told us that we fly kites at Easter to celebrate the fact that Christ rose from the dead. We flew kites because it was fun. The fun started with the making. We made 'nose kites' with a 'bull' that made them sing, delicate little 'kankawas' that danced on the wind and 'girl' kites with long, waving frills. We suffered the pathos of Good Friday and endured the ceremonial of Easter Day because the kites were beautifully ready, and waiting to be flown on Easter Monday.

For weeks we prayed for good weather and woke up early to rush through breakfast and be off to the 'sea' beach with the kites. Those who went early had the pick of the spots – away from the trees, away from the soft mud, a good spread of sand with a clear view. Children who fought each other daily co-operated over kites. Parents who argued about the children buried the argument and helped with the kites. Loops had to be made and remade to be dead centre, tails shortened, balls of twine matched to size of kite, and punctures in the paper quickly mended. There would be shouts of 'hold it', 'loose it', 'higher', 'run' and other instructions given only at this time of year. People, often green with envy at the intricacy and craftsmanship of some, would crowd around the different kites. And then suddenly the atmosphere would be crowded with kites, fluttering, waving, dancing in the breeze. The 'singers' could be heard for long distances and they would be pointed out with pride. Some would be given twine that made them soar far above the trees and others would stay closer to the ground. The higher they went, the further they fell if the twine should break. If they did fall, children searched for miles to rescue and repair them.

There was a gum-cherry or 'pasey' tree near our house and it was easy to pick the cherries. When ripe, they looked like small white grapes but instead of pulp they were filled with a sweet sticky juice very effective for pasting. For the whole of the Easter, we remade, replaced or refurbished our kites but as time passed we flew them with less and less zeal. After about five or six days, our minds would turn to other things, and the kite paper, string and thin rope for tailing would be put away for another year. We pointed out those caught in the trees and, with a weird fascination, watched them disintegrate.

The kites in the shops, or those the older boys sold from door to door, would no longer interest us, and they would simply drop out of consciousness. Even the special one, which had been made with such concern for its form and beauty, would be thrown aside, and when one of my older cousins, consumed with guilt, remarked, 'You can't keep kites, kites don't keep.' I would nod, think of the Easter to come, and say, 'No, kites don't keep.'

I would look out of the window at the mangrove trees that had trapped so many beautiful and precious kites, snatched from their tearful owners by the arrogant wind. But there would only be a piece of string, a handkerchief of bright paper, and a whip of tail to show where love and beauty had once come together in a beautiful kite.

HARVEST

My grandfather gave me some pumpkin seeds when I was about five or six and I planted them at the side of our house. Not long after, a pumpkin vine appeared and made its way along the length of the house. It produced small, bell-shaped, pale orange flowers. Bees visited and pollinated them and I watched as the flowers turned into minuscule fruits that later became larger than my head.

When they had ripened, my grandfather insisted that I picked three out of the twelve we had reaped to take to the church. I carried one, and he took the pair.

The church was usually cold and silent without the services but that Saturday morning it was transformed. Long golden stalks of cane had been lashed to the pillars. Bunches of bananas, plantains and coconuts were braced against the choir stalls. Bags and baskets filled with yams, potatoes and fruit of all kinds could be seen in the most surprising places. Large, succulent guavas, papayas and water melons asserted their presence by colour, size and shape. The altar was a spread of strong, colourful flowers. Brass and furniture polish had been overtaken by the smell of natural things.

'Why market day come to church?' I asked my granddad.

'Harvest,' he replied. 'Not market day. This is God's house and these are God's plants to say thanks.' I did not quite understand, and on the way home he told me the story of Cain and Abel with a new emphasis. I must be honest and say that I preferred the violence because violence was all about me. I could understand it. Parents thrashed children, children thrashed younger ones and animals. Husbands thrashed wives. Harvest was a new idea to me. In giving away the best, supreme unselfishness had to be learned.

My grandparents planted rice each year, long before the Rice Marketing Board was formed. Ankle-deep in water they sowed the seedlings. Each day thereafter one of us was taken along to help scare the birds away. Then at last it was July and the grain was ripe and had to be cut and bundled. What fun it was to be out in the heat of the day, the purpose of the work clearly in the heart and in the eye! We hired oxen to thresh the grain, and took turns to watch them tirelessly and patiently do as they were ordered. The bags of grain stood like rigid, silent sentinels until we collected and counted them. So many for the harvest festival, so many to be milled into rice, so many for the animals, so many for the poor, so many to be sold. My grandfather wished to sell his own rice. He did not want to hand it over to anyone to sell it for him. He and his family had planted it, and watched it grow.

Proudly we took our paddy to the harvest. We sang 'We Plough the Fields and Scatter' with conviction. The church was indeed the place where the whole village acknowledged God's eternal mercies. We believed in miracles and in God, for each day spent among our crops and with our vulnerable selves, undermined what we believed about man.

EXCURSIONS

Excursions, or giant village outings, usually happened on Whit Monday, and were invariably planned by the Burial Society. The members travelled in families, and we were allocated the best seats in the best buses. On the day of the outing, we gathered at the cinema where the convoy of buses waited. My grandfather wore the same outfit for every occasion – straw boater, flannel trousers and black and white shoes. I never associated my grandmother with haute couture, but my grandfather, with his handsome face, was the smartest man there. Life-sense, zest, shrewdness, originality and candour, all these traits were embedded in my grandmother, but clothes never worried her. She always said that what mattered was what went on 'inside' a person. So wherever she went, she wore a long, printed, cotton dress with pockets for her clay pipe, a cotton headscarf and a hat. Her shoes were always very flat heeled. She left the quest for style and elegance to her daughters – and they took both very much to heart. Those going on the outing would be dressed to kill. I can hear them now. 'We mustn't look like country come to town, now. Everything mus' match.' We would all eventually arrive and take our places. As each bus started its journey, there would be cheering, clapping and waving; this would happen again as we passed through villages where people were out front watching and waving to us.

We would sing song after song, the bus going nonstop at breakneck speed. If people thought of accidents they never showed it. I made a very important discovery on an outing – women's breasts shook in response to the movement of the bus. I had to shake my whole body to get my bare chest to move, but they just sat there and their breasts jumped about all on their own. Very, very surprising it was. I began to look forward to the day when I would be grown into a woman with such eloquent breasts.

The journey to the town took about two hours. On reaching there we went to the hall that had been booked for us to eat our plentiful food. My grandfather would whip a 'flattie' of rum from his breast pocket, have a nip and lead the men off to see the sights. My grandmother visited relations and my aunt would hasten to shops that were open, usually to buy sweets and cakes. We would window-shop and compare the cost of material as sold by the Assyrian peddler, Mahmood, with the prices in the 'town' stores. We would walk round the town and, except to try and fleece us, no one would take the slightest notice of us.

At my aunt's house, there would be more to eat, drink and pack away for the journey home. The town-talk, town-ways and town-consciousness of some of the people we visited would irritate me, until at long last we would set off once more to the hall to collect our things, climb into our buses and start the journey home.

It was always a quiet, tedious journey. Because I was so tired, the conversation going on around me would become interminable and even incomprehensible and I suppose I would fall asleep. Suddenly, I would be awakened by the smell of cane on the wind, of rice drying out, of rotting lotus flowers in stagnant water, all running out to greet us. An unspoken look of relief would creep over all faces. The women would wipe their faces with 'pompei' handkerchiefs – the 'pompei' bought by the drop from the local drug store. Those who wore hats would straighten them, and those with 'pressed' hair would comb it through.

There would be a rapid sharing of leftover food. The children would be urged to wake up; and everyone would be quite ready to say what a wonderful time they have had at the excursion.

My grandmother used to say that going on an excursion was like having a baby – the pain was never remembered.

Another year would come round and there we would all be again – same buses, same bags, same refreshment, same journey, same superficial hilarity. But, of course, different clothes.

VILLAGE FUN

The social life of the village centred around the church and the Burial Society. On Whit Monday the church usually gave a 'tea' in the school hall. Tickets were sold over a period of weeks and on presentation of the ticket, the holder was admitted to the tea, which was usually taken wearing best clothes and showing very good manners. We sat at a table dressed in blinding white with china cups, sideplates and cake forks. We were served a portion of cake, a cup of tea, a bun and perhaps sandwiches. It was usually very good value for money since my grandma was always involved. Sometimes there was dancing too. Girls dancing with girls, and boys looking on. Other races attended the teas but, in the main, they celebrated their own, mostly religious functions.

The Burial Society functions were much livelier. Theirs were fetes in the ball-field and shove-downs in the school hall. The shove-downs were great fun. Families and friends formed a line the width of the hall and, followed by other similar lines, danced round and round in a backward-forward motion. There was monumental crowd participation in the singing – so much so that it often caused the folk band to retreat. For all we were worth, we sang:

> Hold your dawg mista
> Hold your dawg
> Bull dog gwine bite me

or:

> Bandoola hold de light
> Leh me see how de money givin' spen' tenight

or:

> All you character gone, gal
> All you character gone.
> Dicky Dum Dicky Dum ah wan to dodo
> Sense all you character gone.
> Fan me sofer berry fan me
> Sense all you character gone.

or:

> Gal ah wha' da da
> Ah me libin
> Oh gal it black an shine
> Ah me libin.

The songs went on and on until, exhausted, we went home. We would be hoarse the next day from shouting shove-down songs.

The soirees were more organised. Uncle Caesar and his band came down from Eversham and he controlled events with a rod of iron. He was small and slight with a cap of downy-white hair. He knew all the songs from way back and played them on his flute. He recited the words and gravely warned us that the band was in charge.

> Last night me bin a Bamboo Dam
> Me see Sityra lay down deh
> Me aks Sityra wha' she a do deh,
> Sityra hice up she frock
> An whine like a Buxton goat

> Sityra mo man deh
> Sityra mo man deh

I loved the soirées for the particular sound of the music, and because my grandparents enjoyed them. There was a kinship with Uncle Caesar that reached far back in time. When he played and sang he released feelings that could only be expressed in a dance that grew out of slavery. The song that told of Auntie Bess crying because her husband had walked from a far plantation to be with her, for just one night, was particularly poignant:

> Hear Auntie Bess!
> Hear Auntie Bess. Ah holler
> E gone! E gone! E gone! Me man
> E gone! E gone! Oh Gado,
> Foreday mornin cock a crow
> Hear Auntie Bess. Ah holler.

I remember the harmonious blending of voices, the deep bass voices of the men forming a backdrop against the piercing harmony of women's voices to articulate the crimes against black families that were at the core of slavery. Today, these songs are being revived, but to me they bring to mind a panorama of people who were part of my childhood.

WEDDINGS

I remember the first wedding I ever attended. The couple had a three year old daughter and we were both flower girls timidly walking behind the bride dressed in virginal white. She had a que-que dance and my grandma took me. Since she made all the wedding cakes in the village, she took me to all the que-que dances and when I should have been in bed, I was out there with the women singing and dancing.

A que-que started simply. A group of women approached the bridehouse and sang:

> Goo' night ... (mother's name) Goo' night oh
> Me come fe tell you goo' night oh.

When the mother emerged and greeted them, they sang and asked:

> Ah who go stan' am
> Ah who go stan' am
> Ah who go stan' half a bottle tonight.

The bride's mother, holding up a bottle of rum replied:

> Ah me go stan' am
> Ah me go stan' half a bottle tonight.

She would hand over the bottle and they would proceed to the site of the que-que where the singing and dancing started in earnest. The que-que dance in my grandmother's time was a graceful, stamping, turning dance. The women always sang the songs in a special order, starting with:

> Me no deady yet
> Me no deady yet bam bam bam
> Me no deady yet
> Me no deady yet can-crow pick me yeye
> Bam bam bam me no deady yet
> Me no deady yet village bell a toll
> Bam bam bam me no deady yet.

Then followed songs like bamboo fire, such as 'Janey Girl' who was bidden to obedience in marriage:

> Oh Janey, Janey Gal
> Do what you mama seh
> Janey Gal
> Do what you papa seh
> Oh Janey Gal – Janey Gal
> Do what you husban' seh.

As the singing proceeded the dancing would come into its own with the 'dancing down'. This was the limbo dance:

> Limba limba limba leh me see you
> Limba like a rainbow
> No so you seh me 'tan' so
> No see you seh me 'tan' so
> I can bruk down iron bedstead.

The woman who could pick up a knotted handkerchief with her teeth would have been the best limbo dancer. Then they would set out to find the bride hidden at home. The que-que would end when she was found, advised about marriage, and given all the money donated by onlookers at the que-que dance.

The church was always decorated for a wedding, and it was of interest to our whole village. The bride chose her bridesmaids and the groom paired them off with his friends – his best men. They would arrive in pairs to the ceremony with the first bridesmaid and best man arriving just before the bride. She would be in the traditional dress to be 'given away' by her father or any other relation. It was a time for cruel comment the dresses, shoes – indeed the entire outfit of the bride's family came in for scrutiny. Their foibles, idiosyncrasies and stupidities would be carefully noticed. The bride's dressmaker came in for the closest scrutiny of all, but if she survived her reputation was made.

After the wedding, there would be the traditional drive through the village and then onward to the reception. Some of these were farcical. If the girl was a virgin she was made to walk on a white sheet and the women danced and sang:

> Mash am gal
> Water deh fo wash am.

On the whole the receptions in our village were straightforward. Both families held receptions with a pink iced cake for the man, and a white iced cake for the bride.

Speeches would be made and the cake 'stuck'. The sticking of the cake was to solicit contributions for the young wife's first days of housekeeping. At this event the 'man of words' came into his own, with a humorous interplay of long, outrageous words expressing felicitations and wishing longevity for the marriage.

The dancing would go on till break of day, with some of the women going home to change dresses two or three times during the festivities. If the girl was from a large and popular family she might be given substantial amounts of money on her wedding day. Most of it would be pinned to her dress or her train. A wedding was of concern to the whole family. Every member, however far removed, contributed to it and it was a time when families would travel miles to be present at the function, were prepared to sleep rough and endure hardship without complaint.

VILLAGE CRICKET

Village cricket matches were usually played on a Sunday afternoon and everybody attended them. We had our own cricket club, formed by the young men of the village. They represented all the different races who lived there and even my uncle, who was slightly lame, played for the club. Even though the temperature was in the nineties, they wore traditional dress, consisting of flannels, blazer, white shirt, soft white plimsolls and cricket cap. The black blazers had S. C.C. – for Skeldon Cricket Club – in gold embroidery on the pockets. Brotherhood and belonging were the sentiments upon which the club was founded. No one talked of race and each unto his own. We were Skeldonians and proud of it. The tentacles of divide and rule had not yet appeared to entangle us. European overseers had no jurisdiction in our village.

When the club played cricket, the whole village played cricket. One match in particular comes back to me. The sun was 'broiling' hot, and for some reason which I cannot recall, I left the house after all the others to attend the match. The village was like an enchanted garden; only the old were there, asleep on the verandahs. The silence was almost overpowering because even on Sundays children shouted across the yards to other children, or parents could be heard summoning their brood from some exploit among the mangroves or on the sand. Everyone had gone to the match and taken their voices with them. It was an important match. An invincible team had come up from Rosehall.

When I arrived, the visiting team from Rosehall were having a very hard time. They were falling like ninepins to the wizardry of our fast bowler, Bachan, a slightly-built, sociable, intelligent, Indian lad, who could make the ball spin like a copper-coin. He had scored a number of successes and everyone was shouting and singing:

> Constantine bowl you bodyline
> Bowl, bowl, bowl, you bodyline

Then the visiting team made a stand and scored some sixes, and straight away some women from our village began to 'cook them' in a pretend obeah cauldron. It was only a prank, but my Aunt Ella and her friend Myra Clark were pretty convincing obeah workers. They leaped and chanted round the pot, uttering magic words and shouting, 'Out-for-nought-leh-e-out-for-nought!' to the delight of us all. By sheer coincidence the batsman was caught out, and the visitors took the prank seriously. Blows followed words and stumps were pulled, until the women stopped the distracting activity of casting spells. Everybody was in stitches because my aunt was harmless and full of fun. She offered to work obeah for the visitors. She picked up some grass and, whirling it into the wind, shouted, 'Mek dem win!' in a deep guttural voice. The game was resumed when the captain of our team persuaded her to stop and enjoy 'cakes and cool drinks' like everyone else. 'Yes', agreed my aunt, 'there's nothing like a full belly to mek the tongue feel sleepy.'

Fresh enjoyment attached itself to whatever was happening. Every time a six was hit, a communal dance around the perimeter of the pitch followed. Every time someone was bowled or caught, gestures of protest were heard. 'Sides' were changed in the fun. 'Grease hand' was shouted when anybody dropped a catch. The children began a mini match on the sidelines, and some people became interested in that, so some of the exuberance was channelled away from the main match.

On the cricket field, the men took on new personalities, fashioning themselves on known Georgetown cricketers. During the week they did horrible, low-paid jobs in field or factory. But when it was time for cricket they became upstanding, proud men, committed to playing in the finest tradition of the game. They had all started to play cricket as soon as they could walk. Wherever the ground was flat enough, or a stick could be found to serve as bat, wherever a green, round fruit, or a piece of balata could be obtained to serve as ball, a game of bat and ball – which would develop into cricket – would start. Girls played too, but never with the same intensity as the boys.

Village cricket brought us all together. It was a time to forget the daily grind and to enjoy ourselves within the boundaries set by our own place, our own space, and within our own culture. The ball, a round object flying through the air, took on symbolic significance. Some saw it as destiny: they faced it squarely. Others took a halfhearted cut at it. Yet others turned it aside and watched its course along the grass.

THE CIRCUS

No-one had ever seen a circus. No-one knew what to expect. But early one morning a convoy of high-sided trucks and caravans raced determinedly down our village street. The word 'KICKAPOO' – which we thought outrageously funny – was painted on the side of each one in very large letters. The convoy turned into the lane leading to the old ricemill, with its large, concreted rectangle of ground. Then the circus people unloaded their suitcases, boxes and brightly-coloured clothes from the parked caravans. After walking round the trucks and looking keenly at them, they went inside one of the houses. It was a very large house owned by some Chinese merchants.

The circus people occupied this house for the rest of their stay. They were an exceptional crowd. Though they were European in full or in part, the children in particular were dirty and unkempt. There were two dwarfs among the several men, one wearing a large-brimmed hat, and several women, one very fat. I stood spellbound. *Our* Europeans, the ones who came into our village from the plantations, were always well-dressed in clean white shirts, khaki breeches and topi. The women were always neat in their plain cotton dresses, with Indian boys walking circumspectly behind them, carrying the purchases they made. Now here was a dirty lot, driving their own vans and shouting at one another and even 'knocking' their children. *Ours* usually kicked the yardboy if their own children annoyed them. We watched these people's every movement.

'They not white people' my cousin said; 'they Portuguese. Look that lady got a big foot.' And sure enough, the last woman to come out of the van had a swollen leg, indicative of filaria which some unfortunate people get from being infected by one species of our mosquitoes. But regardless of the foot she behaved as if she owned everything and everyone.

How it happened I cannot recall, but they bought eggs, chickens and vegetables from us in such large quantities that my grandmother said she was glad they had come.

We discovered that bears, chimps, monkeys, ponies, dogs and an elephant, larger than any animal I had ever seen before, with deeply crinkled skin and banana-leaf ears, were all part of the circus. The bears were enormous too, though the keeper was not the least bit afraid of them. We were fascinated by all they did, and the way the animals were heedful of their keepers' commands.

All day long the men worked with the help of some villagers, to build a platform in the centre of the big top. They also brought some chairs from the cinema and erected plank seats with the wood that had been left there. They sprinkled sawdust to cover the places where the village mud was thick and clinging. Then, to crown it all, they erected a merry-go-round with hard wooden horses who looked at us with painted eyes, and grinned as only wooden horses can. From then on, daily rides were obligatory. The first ride was magical. Round and round I went, lost in the wailing tune, feeling the blended sensations of fear and pleasure, caught up in the warp of experience. Suddenly it was all over and, with the turning sensations still in my head, I was sure I would be swallowed up by the circus.

To our amazement, the bears rode their scooters and danced with the man in the Mexican hat; and the chimp, carrying a monkey on his back, fooled around with the bicycle and, to the delight of us all, threw his boater at the fat man. The tumblers and the juggler cleverly did their acts, though the meanness of the clowns to each other made me so uncomfortable that I wanted to go home.

The strong man and the one of the dwarfs did a flying trick on the trapeze and the little girl stood on the galloping horse. For a thousand pounds, I cannot recall whether the elephant took part in the circus, but I do remember the fortune-teller who came round to offer her skills before the show started, because my grandfather dared her to tell him his name. 'If you can do that, I will pay you to tell the future,' he said.

After each show, they sold us their Kickapoo products, and I persuaded my grandmother to buy some shoe polish, because I was fed up with cleaning my shoes with banana skins. She resisted the Kickapoo Worm Exterminator for Animals though, saying that feeding boiled plantain stems to them was just as good. When they showed her their Kickapoo Caustic Soda, she said that banana ash was just as caustic and dared them to soak their hands in it overnight. She countered all their products with old and tried ones of her own, handed down and down from the slave plantations where black people were really left to their own devices.

Bitter aloes, she told them, was good for sprains; soursop leaf boiled and drunk, for heart troubles; the juice from leaves of the carrioncrow bush was excellent for ringworm and cured it almost overnight. She told them to lick tamarind syrup for coughs and colds, and that the best shampoo in the world was young ochro leaves in pure rainwater.

A little girl brought a monkey, dressed in a little red frock, to shake hands with all the children. 'Tell them that on the last night of the circus, there will be a dancing competition,' she said. The winners would be able to buy Kickapoo products at half price. 'Do you hear that? Now go and tell your family.'

I never saw another circus for thirty years, but I remember the Kickapoo circus so well. It was there that I saw in the flesh, a hulking brown bear, an old, grey elephant, bike-riding monkeys and grunting clothes-dressed chimps, all in a rigged-up tent, many miles from where nature intended them to be.

PART FOUR

THE BRIGHTS

They were 'Brights' in our village but what they did was one of the unanswered questions of my childhood. 'Brights' was the name the villagers gave to the six or seven young women who every day walked up and down our road in a self-conscious cluster. They did not wish to work as domestics for the plantation whites, so they did not work. 'Brights' was a misnomer. Most of the time, the girls were too poor to dress seductively or to be anything but run-of-the-mill in appearance.

Only on Saturday afternoons did they make something of an attempt to tart themselves up. The boldest amongst them dressed as if all the villagers had four-eyes-a-piece and would help them find young men to curl themselves around, like a vine to a tree. Sometimes, one or more of them would get merrily drunk and try to joke with 'respectable' people. Then the uncharitableness of such people would leap out into the light to show the Brights their place.

Two sisters, Adina and Leonora, were said to be Brights. Leonora was a young, petite and pretty girl with laughing dark eyes and a deeply-dimpled face. She was on good terms with life and often came with her sister to talk to my grandmother. Quite suddenly, she died of pneumonia. I spent hours wondering where she had gone and why one so young had simply died. Her sister was inconsolable. Her eyes became even more penetrating and the curl on her beautifully shaped mouth hardly ever materialised into a smile. I remember the day she came to my grandmother, and wept convulsively as they talked. I had to get her a drink of water and then I noticed what beautiful teeth she had. 'I've looked after my sister ever since our father died and now she too is gone,' she said. 'God does not always know best, I think.' I have never forgotten her tears, her voice or her few hopeless words.

Later, she took to holding cumfa or spirit dances to meet up with her people. She advertised them in the market, and people came from other villages to support her. I often wished I could see what actually happened there, but the dances started at about ten o'clock at night and my grandmother never went to them. One had to be a believer and she didn't believe. She explained to all of us that cumfa dancers believed in the Gods of Africans who had perished in slavery, leaving their spirits to roam those seas that had swallowed them up. The cumfa dancers were their kith and kin, placing food and flowers in the river for them. The river would take the gifts to the ocean and the ocean to the open sea. True enough, Adina and her followers came wearing long white robes to cleanse themselves in the river. They would leave offerings of flowers and food in the water and chant strange words until their offerings disappeared out of sight. Later in the evening, the drumming and celebration would start and continue the whole night through. The thumping of the drums made the whole village talk of the cumfa dance. It gave the dancers a status, a selfhood and an identity. I could never imagine what went on, but my aunts told me that Adina danced down the stairs backwards, a glass of water steady on her forehead. She also went into trances and told fortunes.

People were hypnotised by their beliefs about the Brights and made up stories about them, and it was whispered that young men sought 'experience' from them. 'Experience' in the context of the Brights was a mysterious word. I sensed the implications very much later in my late teens when our grocer came to talk to my grandparents about his eldest son. Apparently, the lad had disappeared. His usual haunts yielded nothing of him. And then someone recalled seeing him in deep conversation with one of the Brights.

He was subsequently found hiding behind the fowl coop, trouserless and self-conscious. The Bright demanded five dollars in exchange for the trousers and hurt feelings at 'being approached' by a 'mannish force-ripe child-of-a-boy'.

In every age and place, young men and women feel the stirrings of nature and seek out those who are free to help them express these feelings. Those young women were courageous enough to defy the claustrophobic conventions in which people became trapped. They sought individualism although it meant ostracism within a community which could not allow the expression of individual needs or separate personal from group feelings. In our village, people shared a common opinion, mood or view. The deviants were tolerated but never really accepted unless they toed the community line. In time, the Brights would grow older and get written off as 'women'. Some would have become mothers of children who might choose other ways to show their individuality. Still, the deeds of the Brights were a part of our history and perhaps, in time, their influence would resurface.

NEIGHBOURS

We had East Indian neighbours on both sides of us. On the right were the Muslims. I remember old Maka and his wife Mai. He was tall and gaunt, with a foot-long, pointed white beard. Mai was fat and comfortable to talk with. As he was impatient, so she was patient. They were shopkeepers and used to let us buy a pennyworth of currants if we had only a penny. Their four grandchildren, only one a boy, were always swapping onions with us for cakes and corn-bread. We ate the onions just like any other fruit. One day the mother of the children died and their lives changed dramatically. They had a succession of stepmothers and became strangers to us. The boy subsequently went out of his mind, and the girls married far away from our village.

On the left of us were the Hindus, Ram and Dasi. They were great fun, friendly, generous and talkative. They were always coming in with queries about their animals and their plants. Ram farmed up the river and brought us bags of cocerite, awara and genip, bread-nut and delicious mamee apples. Sometimes Dasi made puri and called us in to eat with her. My aunts used to read and write for them. They had a fat daughter called Matia, who quite suddenly got married one day. It was a real Hindu wedding with lots of food and ritual. All the cooks were men. They cooked a great deal of food which they served on plantain leaves.

Behind them lived Beeda, a dear old soul, who kept house for her tall, quiet son called Tull. Her elder son had gone to America, and sent her money every month in a letter. The whole village knew what a dutiful and attentive son he was. Her house was dark and cold inside and smelled of eastern spices. She, too, was illiterate, but Tull was half-schooled. He was a silent, creepy man. I used to go down to the beach with Beeda and help her collect crab-seed, the seed of the crabwood tree which was thrown on the beach by the tide. What she did with the seeds I cannot now recall, but sometimes she sold crab-oil and, on reflection she must have made it from the large fleshy seeds.

On the last day of each month, the postman delivered her letter. She received it dressed in her best skirt and bodice, which she called her 'jhickit' and her best, coloured voile orhni. Even now I can recall her clean, oiled feet, contrasting with the ground, as she stood waiting for the postman. Her hands were always crossed low in front of her to quieten the circles of silver bangles she wore. Her clothes reflected the regard in which she held her son across the sea. If the letter missed its usual delivery, there she was again the next day, confident of receiving it. When Tull eventually disappeared to 'live home' with a woman villages away, she carried on just the same. Nothing changed. Still neat and tidy to receive her letter, she continued to share her good fortune with the village children. She searched deep in her pocket and fished out 'sugar-babies' and crystallised sugar candies for us. My grandmother sold her corn for her hens and other people bought the eggs they laid. She was happy, smiling and talking in her quiet way, giving me advice about the rag dolls I made and telling me constantly that my pet goat was not to be encouraged in the house.

One sad month, her letter missed its day. She waited for the postman the next day and the next. The letter did not come. The furrows on her brow deepened. She insisted that the postman made sure, doubly sure. There was no letter. The pressure on the postman eventually caused him to avoid her. There were no sweets for us, so we too avoided her. For some unknown reason we ran squealing when we saw her. She had suddenly become somebody unworthy of friendship. She refused the corn my grandmother offered her on credit and her hens laid tiny eggs which displeased the buyers so much they paid her less for them. She lost interest in her appearance. Her clothes got dirtier and dirtier. She lost, also, her sense of time and waited for the postman at the end of the day although he called around eleven each morning. The letter continued to fail her. The days became a week and then a fortnight. She burst into our house in a state of great distress. 'Me son mussy dead. Me son mussy forget me.' My grandmother went through the possibilities and the probabilities with her. She remained inconsolable. 'Me son mussy tek wife. Wife mek man forget mudder.' She would not eat. Finally, she took to her bed.

My grandmother called on her and I went too. She had a high fever, my gran said, and put cold towels steeped in limewater on her head. She was persuaded to sip tea and soup. She looked wan and very tired. She turned her face to the wall and curled herself up with her aches and her fears. She grew thin and everyone predicted her imminent death.

Three weeks later the letter came. There had been a strike of stevedores in Georgetown and the mail from abroad could not be unloaded, and then sent on to their destinations by train. My aunt read the letter to her and she got out of bed. Later that day she tottered to the post office to cash her postal order. None of the children could face her.

She never spoke to us again or went further than her doorstep. She neglected her hens and waited for the postman inside her house, although she still put on her best things.

She spoke only to my grandmother. Months later, when she died, my grandmother insisted that waiting so anxiously for the late letter had killed her, but our children's laughter had helped. It drove the poison of unworthiness into her heart.

A FEAST

The sow, her ear twitching, lay in her corner of the large pen. From time to time she grunted gently, as if to reassure the piglets, each clinging to a teat on her light-black underbelly. There was no teat for the extra one. Those rooting for her milk unconsciously squashed him or straddled him. Too hungry to resist, he mewed weakly, and with his eyes closed and his head only slightly bobbing, he rooted in the dry, crisp tufts of grass, meant for maternity bedding. He was small and crinkled and his back looked as if it had been painted bright pink by an indifferent hand.

'Drown that pig,' my grandmother said. I hesitated. 'Go on, drown it. It wouldn't live. If too many pigs, kittens or puppies come, it better to drown some. He is a "runty", no good for anything.' I took the piglet and was surprised at how warm it felt. I put a hessian bag around it and hid it in the oven. The piglet would be safe in there. My grandmother would not use the oven for a few days. It was a safe, dark and warm place. I got some food for the piglet and fed it. The squashed up cocoa and cassava bread seeped out of the corner of its snout but it sucked my finger. It was a strange sensation. I soaked a piece of cloth in the cocoa, wrapped it firmly round my finger and the pig really sucked. I gave a little scream of pleasure. My grandmother walked in and caught me – oven door open, pig in hand. She was surprised to find the piglet still alive, and to hear it sucking shocked her so much that it instantly became a little baby, helpless and delicate and worthy of her attention, her care and her cures. She fed it with an eyedropper and then with a bottle and a home-made canvas teat. This was just a closely rolled two-inch piece of canvas stitched in place, and with a small hole in the middle. The piglet began to improve.

Its two beadlike eyes stayed open for longer and longer periods. A kind of strength pervaded its thrusting and wiggling. Then it stood up and one day it ran. It ate all the scraps people threw at it and it grew. I measured its circumference with a piece of string, a vine-rope, a belt and with my wooden hoop which I bowled along as I ran my errands. The pig was more interesting than any dog and many times more entertaining than any cat. I loved my pig, although I could never tell if it returned my love. A piercing look came into its beady eyes and its snout twitched and leaked when I approached with its food. We freed it from its tether and it roamed around. It pillaged the kitchen, got kicked, squealed and got kicked some more. It was a house-pig. A pet. One day, all that suddenly changed.

Two Madrasis came into the yard – an old man with a hairy face and carrying a long stick in one hand and a limp hessian bag in the other, leading a younger and friskier man. They asked for 'Mistah Jems', my grandfather. They whispered to each other. My grandmother joined them and they whispered to her but she said out loud, 'I know what you want. Not too little, not too big, a good pig. When is your feast?'

'Des apanoon, Missy,' the old man said in an obsequious tone. 'We want de pig, right now, dis clock, dis time.'

They strode into the recesses of the yard and the next thing I heard was my pig being bundled squealing into the old man's bag.

My grandfather saw the look of despair on my face. 'The pig too big. It too much trouble. We have to sell it,' he said. 'The sanitary inspector said to sell it.'

By now the men were almost out of the yard. The pig wriggled and squealed in the bag, making it slip off the old man's shoulder. The younger man took one end and between them they carried it out to their cart. I found myself walking and then running behind them. They turned into the road that led to my aunt's house and stopped on some waste land within two hundred yards of it. I watched them from the kitchen window. People had already assembled for the party. There were pots and pans, music, and children in bright shirts and dresses. Smoke came in gusts from a large ground-fire. Women prepared massala and spices on their grinding stones. One young girl, whom I knew quite well, beat the drum and another danced a whirling dance, while the bells on their ankles jangled in a pleasing and merry manner. I heard the pig squeal – one, two, three times. The men laid the carcass on a piece of wood and poured boiling water over it. The bloody water trickled down on to the ground as they scraped off its sparse black hair. It took them a long time to prepare the carcass for cooking. Nevertheless, I waited. They hung it from a nearby tree for some time, then they took it down, flavouring it with Eastern spices and finally stuffing it. I watched, like a sinner waiting to enter hell. At last they wired it up to a spit which the children took turns to work. They sang a jerky song which caused them to jerk the handle of the spit. After a time the most delicious smell rode over the wind and the fat dropping into the fire caused a forest of tiny spluttering flames that have branded my memory to this day. Sometime later they prodded it. One of the women said, 'E done cook. Leh it cold out.' My pig sat there. I imagined it alive only hours before. Suddenly the old man cut into the meat and then the others joined in. The nimble young man bit into a huge piece. As he chewed I could see all the fat glistening on his face. I began to cry and vowed that no one, no one ever would ignore my feelings again.

    I was indifferent to my grandmother for a long time and then the floods came. We saw a helpless little goat standing on a tree trunk as it floated downstream. My grandmother saved it and when no one claimed it, she gave it to me. For a time, it healed my sense of loss, but I have never had a pet like that 'runty' piglet. In life, its antics amused me – in death, its aroma made me feel very hungry indeed.

EARACHE

The shower had subsided and the whips of lightning which had lashed the skies moved on to another place. The trees dripped crystal beads of rain much more slowly now, and skies as blue as a backraman's eyes appeared from under clouds that scurried away, as if ashamed of spoiling a day that had broken so clear and clean.

Out of nowhere they came. A cloud of them. Fat and creamy-white, with glazed, transparent wings. Very much too small for beetles and much too small for houseflies, they turned out to be flying ants which had taken off on their marriage flight, as they did at this time of year and just after a shower of rain. They were attracted to me, I believe, by the all-hailing smell of the macassar oil which my grandmother had put on my freshly-combed hair. It was the holidays and she had combed in star-shaped 'long plaits' to last for the whole month. The ants took over my head. I brushed them off determinedly. But they were determined too. They did not sting. They just scuttled, rummaged and investigated the recesses of my plaits, and then flew off again, frenzied in their search for a mate. I pulled the dead ones out of my hair.

We should not have been under the trees anyway. My grandmother had warned us to keep away from the trees but we had made other plans. Only the day before we had made slingshots, as we called our home-made catapults. They kept us occupied for the long month of August. We made them out of a small forked stick. At the end of each prong we tied a flat, foot-long piece of rubber, joined at the free end by a rectangle of leather which folded over and so contained the shots, made from sun-dried mud pellets. We held the shots in place, stretched the rubber and fired! Slingshots were deadly weapons to birds, lizards, and ripe fruit.

Little bands of us roamed the village, looking for fruit trees. Being a little girl it was quite in order for me to follow my older cousins, and my job was to sneak into the yards and pick up the fruit that they knocked down. It was not necessary to be able to tell the wild from the cultivated. If fruit was plentiful, the children could pick some. We knew whose yards had jamoon, psidium, sapodillas and guava trees. We knew where to find golden apples, genips and paddoo, and if the monkey-apples and cashews growing wild by the seaside were ripe enough to 'knock'. We looked for buru-buru, and see-me-too (passion fruit) as well as a foul-tasting nut called bread-and-cheese in the thick shrubbery by the side of the road.

We were lucky that day. Because of the wind and the rain that had come earlier, a large soursop had dropped to the ground. Soursop had to be eaten with sugar, milk and lime juice added, or else it turns black after exposure to the air, and tastes sickly on its own. One of the group ran off to set up all the prerequisites for a soursop feast, and the rest of us sat down to await his return. It was then that I felt the fluttering in my ear. I must have said something as one of my very much older cousins drove me off. They frequently chased me away. I was not going to spoil their fun by questions, questions, not if the one who behaved like the queen had anything to do with it. My grandmother used to refer to her as Missis Grudgeful, and tell me to be wary of her. All the way home I could feel the fluttering deep down inside my ear and then, moments later, the stabbing pain. I went into the kitchen. There was nobody about. But I had seen my grandmother treat all sorts of everyday illnesses. Out of my unconscious came the realisation that I could help myself. I got some rain water and poured it into my ear. It did not quite go in. I tried again. The fluttering came with much greater energy and the pain grew in size. Water ran down the side of my face.

In desperation I tried the water again. Much more carefully this time. I could feel it going right inside. The fluttering came with much less energy but the pain in a gigantic wave. The stories my cousins had told me of those evil, tricky night-creatures called

Adopi, who made their homes inside people's bodies, and could be heard yickering and conversing at will, flooded my mind. My grandfather had convinced me that it was all nonsense but where was that conviction now? In a state of deep anguish, I laid my head on the kitchen table, throbbing ear down, to try and overcome that heaviness of feeling caused by water in the inner ear.

I must had dozed off. I suddenly became conscious that the fluttering had stopped and with it the pain. My head felt steadier. Water ran out my ear with the sound of air trapped in a shell. Something stuck to my ear lobe. Was it an Adopi's finger, foot or toe? I touched it. It was an ant, dressed for its funeral in earwax. I could have killed it, but death should come only once.

My grandmother came in. She had been told I had the earache. I told her about the pain, and the water, and finally the ant. 'Good girl,' she said. 'Next time, pour in some warm coconut oil to finish off with.' And she started peeling cassava for the evening meal.

THE BLACK BULL

As children we were always warned about animals, especially billy goats, bulls, snakes, guinea fowls and turkey cocks. Guinea fowl, if they were broody, it was said, sometimes blinded children by pecking at their eyes, and goats and bulls were known to use their horns viciously too.

So, we were told to poke sticks rather than our hands into holes, to run in a zig-zag if a nesting alligator should chase us, and to climb a tree to get away from bulls and goats, even though goats climbed too. It was said that the unyielding spine of alligators made them clumsy on land. Fortunately I was never able to put their running ability to the test.

We had gone guava-hunting, my cousin Sydney, my friend Ioleen and I. We chatted light-heartedly as we walked along the path to the place where guavas grew plentifully. Suddenly we heard a sound – like women pounding boiled plantains to make fu-fu. Before we could remark on the sound, a black bull had begun tramping out of the bush growing on the parapet and was heading for us. It bellowed and pounded the ground, its eyes flashing with fury. It rushed steadily on.

We screamed and ran. 'Climb something! Them trees yonder!' my cousin shouted. 'It coming!'

There were only calabash trees. Not very tall, but strong and laden with large, heavy gourds. We managed to climb up. If I stretched my foot down I could touch the bull's back. My sandals stared up at me. I had to slip them off to climb the tree. The bull peed at the base of our tree.

'It marking the place,' my cousin shouted as he crossed over from his tree to ours.

We disconsolately watched the bull and all its antics. To get a gourd we would have had to cut it off the branch, and use both hands to hurl it at the bull, which angrily continued to snuffle and to paw the ground. The basket lay broken on the path and I could see my cousin's catapult dangling from the broken handle.

The bull butted the main stem, the tree shook and the wasps left their smooth, mud-caked nest and investigated. They soon settled down again but something else had been disturbed. Ioleen screamed.

'Look! A snake!'

'Don't be stupid,' said my cousin. 'It's a greenhead. They don't carry poison.'

We watched as the snake writhed off into the grass, its head a pale clean green and its whip of a body silver in the sunlight.

We heard sounds coming from the canal on the right side of the path. The canal on the left was empty of all but dirty water. We started to shout.

'Help! Help! A bull want to kill ah we!'

As the punt came closer we saw three people. Two young men were happily sitting on the bundles of cane it carried. An older man walked beside the mule, all the while hitting it with a thick stick to make it go faster.

'Help! Help!' we shouted.

The two young men gestured rudely to us and went on their way.

'It's that red collar on your dress, Ioleen,' my cousin accused.
'The bull didn't even see it,' she protested.
'How you know! You ask it? Go and ask it.'

The bull bellowed again and thumped the tree. The sun was now at its zenith. Perhaps the creature would feel thirsty and wander off. It didn't. It sat in the shade surveying our tree and watching our every move – chewing its cud and mooing turns about.

'Bulls go to sleep?' I asked no one in particular.

'Trust you to talk foolish!' Sydney replied. 'Everything sleep, even fish and snake.'

Stories of the creatures of the bush began to creep out of my mind with the dying sun. I would surely fall out of the tree if I fell asleep. Then what!

I began to scream for help, hysterical at the thought of being gored by the bull or taken to the land of the undead by ghosts. But apart from the buzzing of wasps and muffled breathing of the bull, there was no sound of anyone else who would come and help us.

'They going to come and find us,' Ioleen said. 'My sister and my ma will come. You 'fraid for dark night?'

'My grandma and my gran...' I began. Then I heard voices – women's voices – clearly and suddenly. All three of us screamed 'Help!' in unison.

'The bull going to kill ah we. Help! Help!'

'The black bull waiting to trample ah we!' yelled Ioleen after we'd stopped screaming.

Surprised, the women put down their batches of wood and pulled long stakes out of them. Waving them and shouting, they crossed the canal.

'Moo,' replied the bull, its eyes flashing with rage. The women's shouting and abuse left it no other option. It retreated hurriedly down the facing parapet, crossed the canal and disappeared.

When at last we did get home, we had to face the music. We had overstayed our time and had no guavas to give to my aunt for her jam. We told her our story. My hands were swollen from the pressure of holding on to the tree. One of the women came later to see if we had got licks and to beg for us not to be punished. 'Climb a tree,' everyone advised us yet again.

'What if it had a wasp nest?' I asked.

'Trust you to talk foolish!' scolded my aunt. My cousin and I exchanged glances. That night I had my first nightmare. I climbed high walls and trees, flew for miles, swam rivers and finally fell into a dungeon. As I floated up to daylight there was the black bull waiting to gore me to bloody bits.

'Moo!' it bellowed as it tossed its horns.

'Trust you to talk foolish,' I replied.

SCHOOL

When I was four or five, I used to go to a school called St Cuthberts – when I wanted to. It was run by a relation of mine and I was taught by a spinster who mistakenly believed in her ability to teach. I got hit for doing my sums wrong. I hated school. I remember, though, going on Tuesdays when they chanted 'Twenty rules and maxims' and on Thursdays when they did drawing. I chose a picture from a pile and drew it. I chose 'Dutch Flagon', a weird drinking cup, every Thursday, and drew it. Then I went home. I attended regularly for practice for the concerts and Empire Day celebrations. Afterwards, I stayed at home, happy to go a-back dam with my grandparents, feed the turkeys and poultry, write my poems and stories, play with my goat or read the books which were in the house. The regimentation of the school was stifling. I always had to think what the teacher wanted me to think, when, and where, why and how much. They beat children too – especially if they went late. Since I did not really want to go, I often went late. The latecomers were chased round the school, the headmaster lashing out at their legs with a long leather strap. I ran home if I was lashed. I gained little by going to school. I loved geography – especially physical geography. I read as much as I could about all the things which interested me and learned to look and see. My grandfather bought me a 'Geikie' geography book which contained everything about the world, the tides, the sun – all that interested me.

As I grew older, my grandfather said I had to go to the church school if I was to be confirmed. At twelve years old, or thereabouts, I changed school. All through the following five years going to school was the worst experience of my childhood. I won prizes for all sorts of subjects: Poetry, English, Originality, Handwriting and Best Reader, but in terms of days, I did the fewest of all my contemporaries in the traditional school. My childhood was self-organised, with a little guidance from my grandparents, who loved me as much as, years later, my husband was to do. I hated school and told everyone so.

But – school never got hold of my inquisitiveness or my creativity or deadened my will to learn. I have always created my own interests. I didn't have to put up with a succession of garrulous, babbling teachers – only four in a whole lifetime. Two were exceptional men. But I liked school no better. I still hate the idea of compulsory school for every child. My two children went to school as little as possible in their early years, when I taught them how to think, make choices and stick with them and learn for themselves what affects validity of belief, thought and action. They are two successful people with a formidable array of self-learned skills. School is an institution which can institutionalise children's thinking.

Oh yes, so when, many years later I became a headteacher, I was determined that the school would be one which focused on children's interests, be one to which children freely wanted to come, and enjoyed being there. For over fourteen years I worked to achieve that.

FEAR

I had never heard anyone speak of menstruation or witnessed its manifestations at home. Although I had two female cousins just older than I, they never told me. Anything to do with body products was obscene talk. On reflection, I had heard one, who was a little gauche, always being reminded of the fact that she wasn't a child any more. I recall her eyes lowered in shame, and the stance of disgrace that she would self-consciously assume as a result of that reprimand.

I must have been fourteen the day I noticed the dark red smear on my bloomers with the elasticated legs. The smear of blood bothered me, but the ignorance in which I had been kept almost made me die of fear. As usual, I had been catching ladybirds from the blacksage bushes from which we broke the choicest branches to make chewsticks. (We cleaned our teeth with the chewed end of the stick.) When I felt the sudden clamminess, I had to let go the ladybirds and have a look. I have been running, climbing, and jumping high for fruit. The sight of the smear threw me into a spin. Perhaps I had broken some vital organ deep down inside me. Yet again, I wished that I was transparent and could simply undress and watch how my body worked. The postmaster, I recall, had a skeleton clock. One had only to look to see the parts moving relentlessly round and round.

I made my way back to the pond along a muddy path, with footprints still showing water from the rain that had previously fallen. Surreptitious looks about me revealed no one in sight. I soaked my knickers as best I could without taking them off, and them attempted to squeeze out the water. Little streamlets ran down my legs and my calves. I dried the water with some grass that stuck to me without having much effect. I walked home worried out of my mind. There it was again – a round, bright red spot the size of a half-crown. Surely this is death, I thought.

I complained of feeling unwell and went to bed early. In bed I itemised my few possessions against the names of the friends whom I wanted to inherit them. Then I thought a great deal about death and dying, heaven and earth, and how crabs felt when they were boiled, and how fishes felt when they were fried. My thoughts were jumbled – old and young – child and adult – black, white and grey. I was a solitary child growing more and more to dislike the values I was being offered within my family. The emphasis upon clothes and the external self, the right of relations to pry, interfere and control, my own inability to understand the metaphysical world, my reluctance to be other people's person. I worried too about work – what would I be in the future? What would I do? There were very few people around whom I could respect or look up to. In my community, education seemed to touch on respectability but not on morality.

My grandmother had done the best she could. My grandfather had insisted that I go to school regularly and attend to learning. 'You don't need the teachers,' he said, 'you need to go to school to get confirmed, to read books, to show just how clever you are.'

I realised that I was small, and the world big. I had taken to drawing map after map of the world, noting all the rivers, the continents, the mountains and the seas.

The more I read and drew and learnt, the more inadequate and confused I felt. I had started to feel ugly and fat, although I only weighed six stone. I hunched up when I walked because I noticed two little buttons growing in my breasts. Once I had wished for instant coconut-sized breasts so that they could bump and shake under my dress, just like the women's on the bus. Now it was happening gradually, and along with other things. I decided that death in the morning would be the best for me. I felt a certain sorrow at leaving my grandparents, and despair at being unable to reverse death made me curl up and wait for it.

And then, suddenly, there was the sun streaming in at the window. The birds were singing outside and the world was as clear as rainwater. I sat up in bed happy that confusing yesterday had become a hopeful today. Then I noticed it. The smear had become a flow. There was blood everywhere. I was rigid with fear. I screamed. In came my mother, my grandmother and one of my aunts. They shoved one of my male cousins out of the room. They whispered dramatically among themselves, and then they left me to my mum. 'Now be careful with boys', she said, as if boys were snakes or delicate china. She said nothing more. Dressed up and self-conscious, I went to school. None of the other girls had spoken about their menstruation so I sat mine out too. No hopscotch, climbing, running of jumping for me in case my wretched secret came out. Nobody said that once a month I would have what I discovered was referred to as 'dem tings' and that it was a burden that lasted many years. I just lay there sweating with fear – not knowing that my childhood had fled. I realised *that* years later on.

I often wonder what other girls were told and how they coped. Did they experience fear to the same extent that I had done? What was it that kept us so completely unable to talk about our bodies? Perhaps it was shame that we had become powerless women, at the mercy of men. I pushed that thought aside. I was going to find a wonderful, handsome, generous husband. And I did.

OF TIME AND THINGS

At one end of our village, there was a huge, spreading tree, gnarled with age and time. Its roots rose out of the ground like a monstrous, many-limbed creature, trying to break out of the bowels of the earth. It was the hanging tree in slave days and if it could have spoken it would have told of the cruelties and inhumanities it had seen. It did, though, give sanctuary to the birds in its filigree crest of spreading leaves.

We called it the Big Tree, to give it distinction. It marked the end of the road and, at different times of the day, it became a place where disputes were settled, contracts made and pledges given. It marked where ordered activity ended and haphazard stirrings began. Beyond it, the road sneaked into neglect and incidental desolation. It looked down on a long ditch full of dark, stagnant water in which a thick growth of lotus lilies flourished. The flower heads dropped into the water, rotted and made it smell. And that smell seemed to weave itself into the tree, giving it yet another quality of timelessness and veridicality. It showed its age, and people regarded it with the respect due to old age.

Under it, young men played draughts and dominoes and old men talked of old times; girls dressed in their fineries walked in its shade as if seeking its approval, and young children played hopscotch, skipping and ring-games. The tree was at the end of my village, but strangely it was the centre. There news grew legs and gossip grew wings but many were content just to enjoy its beauty and the mottled shadows it threw when the time was right. We had plenty of time.

Time appeared to spread out before us like a sheet on the grass and we never failed to litter it with our interests and our activities. We had a problem with time. We stretched for our wanderings, our work, our school and our games, but it was never enough.

We played cricket using sticks or pieces of wood for bats, and baby coconuts and mango seeds for balls. We played marbles and marble-games too. A favourite of all the children was 'Nine Holes'. A row of three shallow holes an equal distance apart was scooped out of the sand, and the task was to enter each hole three times, i.e. counting up to nine. Failure brought attack by other players, who frustrated the effort to enter the hole by knocking the marble in any direction. 'Nine Holes' called for skill, concentration, co-ordination and judgment. We also played 'Bounce and Span', in which we bounced our marbles from a low, flat wall. If they landed so close they would be spanned, and buttons to an agreed number had to be forfeited. We played ring-games, rounders, and running games like 'Catcher' and 'Poor'. We took play so seriously sometimes we became as deaf as tortoises to reason and good sense.

We were never bored and lost no time dropping arguments to go sweet-water fishing, or shrimping or catching crabs.

During the month of August, the crabs 'marched'. It was an extraordinary sight to see great numbers of land crabs on the march. In answer to some irresistible inner force, they vacated their holes on land, and scuttling and sneakily yickering, headed for the river. They seemed to be hypnotised by the need for this journey, and regardless of the danger from predators and men with a taste for the delicacy known as crab-back, and for crab-soup and crab-curry, on and ever onward they came. They got scooped up by the basketful until disgust with crab meat caused us to ignore them. My grandfather said they were going to the river to lay their eggs, but all I can remember about them is their little stick-eyes, which never seemed to see any danger, the rapidity of their scuttling and the little flurries of sand that they threw up to the wind.

There was time, too, to pick fruit, and to climb for the sheer pleasure of climbing and to run because there was space to hurl oneself into. There was time to realise that one's world is where significant people and significant events occur. As we take the road to selfhood, we walk on, but every once in a while we look back upon the things which have been and the times which have passed. The past, whatever it is, remains our core. We may be upholstered and even insulated against its reassertion, but it is there just the same.

FIRST STORIES

I was always extremely competitive. I adored winning and never bothered about the size or age of the other competitors. The Negro Progress Convention, at that time a nationwide movement, had established a branch in our village and, besides fundraising to send a young woman called Vesta Lowe to the Tuskegee Institute in America to study Nutrition, the N.P.C. encouraged black pride. The visitors from town used to tell us about the lynchings in the south of America, about Mr Malan and his persecution of black people in South Africa and about Marcus Garvey who was going to take blacks back to Africa. My family were great talkers and a lot of people dropped into our yard to discuss politics. As a matter of fact, everyone of any consequence in our village was black – the doctor, the Anglican priest, the schoolmaster, the postmaster who walked through our village every evening carrying his alarm clock, the sergeant of police, the druggist, both the beef and pork butchers and everyone else I knew. (I always wondered about P.M. Grif and his clock, and then learned that he had a mistress in our village. He needed the alarm clock to wake him up so that he could be on time for the mail-car.)

P.M. Grif had many books and the members of the N. P. C. borrowed them. The N.P.C. encouraged us to read *Up From Slavery,* the autobiography of Booker T. Washington, the poems of Paul Lawrence Dunbar and other great American writers. We also read the proverbs published annually in the magazine which Booker Brothers distributed free of charge.

Sometimes the Negro Progress Convention workers arranged competitions for us, encouraging us to write about the plants and animals around us, and to record stories that our relatives told us. We won little prizes, lead pencils with rubbers, yo-yos, sweets etc. If I live to be a hundred I will never feel the same pride and pleasure that I did when I won my first prize. I had written two stories and I won two prizes – a silver sixpenny piece and a pencil. I wrote a story, 'Why Keskidee Has a White Feather Band Round His Head' and 'How Dumpidu Became King of the Watutsis'. I used to sit and talk with Mrs Mentore, a thin, old-old woman, her face like a sun-dried boulanger and not a single tooth in her head. But she told the most wonderful stories and called herself a Watutsi.

My story was funny: it was about a bird, Keskidee, who was like a saga-boy, flying here, flying there, and living by giving ladies the talk:

One day Blue Saki said, 'Buddy boy, Keskidee boy, you hear the story. War gwine come. We all ha fe go.'

'Who want go must go! War go ruffle me feathers. Deh so smooth. Deh so bright. Deh so nice. That's why I holler Kes-Kidee when I hang from the washing line. I like everybody fe see underneath me belly. Keskidee!' He did some extra tricks and flew off.

Blue Saki went straight to the Old Witch to tell him the story. Old Witch flew to John Crow, to tell him the story. John Crow could not wait to go and tell Chicken Hawk. Chicken Hawk passion raise and he go with the big mouth and his hurtful passion to tell the eagle – king of the birds.

Early day-dawn they woke up and hid in a coconut tree to wait for Keskidee to hang from the washing line and bawl out, 'Kes-ki-dee – see me, Kes-kes-ki-dee.'

Eagle flew down and caught him.

'Keskidee, soldier man, you goin to war and story done!'

'No! No!' Keskidee yelled. 'I sick – see me head. Ma tie kerchief soak in bay rum round my head. Oh God, I too sick! Kes-ki-dee! If you want, kill me! Me head will nevah cool off.'

True, Keskidee did have a kerchief tied round his head to keep it cool. So Eagle flew round and called all the birds to a meeting. They all started to talk and insult Keskidee.

'He too lazy!' they said. 'He is a lazy no-good, not-working talk-mouth.'

'Cool down everybody! Cool down,' shouted Eagle. Everybody fell quiet as mice. Then Eagle asked:

'Kes-Kes, you sick?'

'Yes, too bad!'

'Kes-Kes, you wearing kerchief?'

'Yes. Ma put it on me head'

'Well, Kes-kes, you must wear it all you life. When you hang upside down or fly from tree to tree, you must shout out your name so that people can hear you before they see you.'

'No, ' said Keskidee. 'I will not. Jumbie will tek me name!'

'Then me and Kyat will eat you,' said Eagle.

'No – don't eat me. I will do wha' you want forever and ever and ever.' So Kyat put up his knife-and-fork claws and Eagle hide up his talons.

As a teacher of young children I told that story endlessly and it became a popular one among teachers. Now many people claim it. I won a prize for it – a silver sixpence which I still have.

My other story was about Dumpidu:

Dumpidu had sixty brothers, for his father had many wives. His father was a Chief who lived in a palace made of mud. In his father's palace everyone was happy. But then one day the Chief died of his age. It was not a nice time for Dumpidu and his brothers. Only one could live. Only one could be King. So all the old people, called Elders, gathered and brought a gourd and put it on a table made of grass.

'Whoever can lift this gourd up and drink from it, is the rightful king.' the Elders said.

'How can a man drink if the gourd is empty?' asked the brothers. The Elders watched as one by one they tried to lift the gourd. None could. At last only Dumpidu was left. He was a hunchback. He was ugly. He was not brave and the gourd grew heavier as each man failed to lift it.

The brothers tried to prevent him from approaching the gourd but the Elders insisted. He walked towards the gourd, his hand trembling, his face covered with sweat. At last he reached the grass table and got hold of the gourd. It did not resist him. It came readily into his hand and it was as light as a feather, yet full of sweet water.

A cry went up. Dumpidu was the rightful heir. He grew tall, he grew handsome. He grew strong. He sat on the grass throne and his brothers called him King.

'The law says you must kill your brothers,' said the Chief Elder.

'I will not kill them but will let them travel to other parts of the world.' To show his honesty he told the Elders to show the sweet water to the sunlight.

That night the slave-catchers came and brought all the brothers to this country. That's why Berbicians are proud. They are the children of princes.

LONG TIME 'TORY

    When me remember long time 'tory
Water run a me yeye
    When me remember long time 'tory
Water run a me yeye

    Gal leh me lone, leh me lone
I ent gat nobady
    Gal leh me lone, leh me lone
I ent gat nobady

    Twenty Berbicians down by the cake shop
Not a cent to buy bread
    Twenty Berbicians down by the cake shop
Not a cent to buy bread

    Gal leh me lone, leh me lone
I ent gat nobady
    Gal leh me lone, leh me lone
I ent gat nobady

    Gal leh me lone, leh me lone
Coc'nut milk ah me tea
    So shake Bandori, shake Bandori
Coc'nut milk ah me tea

Also by Beryl Gilroy

Green Grass Tango

Alfred Grayson, a retired and widowed civil servant, decides to buy a dog to try 'not to be so lonely'. Sheba is his passport to the richly multi-racial community of dog-walkers and bench-sitters who meet in a down-at-heel London park. Here Grayson engages with cunning Finbar, theatrical Arabella and her absurd tango-dancing sidekick Harold Heyhoe, Jamaican Maryanne tortured by her demons, Rastafarian Rootsman, old Uncle Nat from Sierra Leone, tattoed Judy and abandoned Lucy.

Grayson, originally from Barbados, has passed for white and kept his origins quiet during his civil service career. But when he tries to befriend Maryanne and she remains suspicious, thinking him English and white, he begins to rethink his past.

In the park, characters, who would not otherwise meet, make unlikely alliances and feel able to expose various identities, or in Alfred's case begin to reconstruct one. Both park and characters have their times of shabbiness and moments of blooming glory.

This is comedy filled with a sense of human fragility and impermanence.

Price: £8.99
ISBN: 1 900715 47 3

Inkle and Yarico
being the narrative of Thomas Inkle concerning his shipwreck and long sojourn among the Caribs and his marriage to Yarico, a Carib woman.

As a young man of twenty, Thomas Inkle sets out for Barbados to inspect the family sugar estates. On the way he is shipwrecked on a small West Indian island inhabited by Carib Indians. He alone escapes as his shipmates are slaughtered, and is rescued by Yarico, a Carib woman who takes him as, "an ideal, strange and obliging lover." So begins an erotic encounter which has a profound effect on both. Amongst the Caribs, Inkle is a mere child, whose survival depends entirely on Yarico's protection. But when he is rescued and taken with Yarico to the slave island of Barbados, she is entirely at his mercy.

Inkle and Yarico is loosely based on a "true" story which became a much repeated popular narrative in the 17th and 18th centuries. Beryl Gilroy reinterprets its mythic dimensions from both a woman's and a black perspective, but above all she engages the reader in the psychological truths of her characters' experiences.

As an old man, Inkle recalls the Carib's stories as being like 'fresh dreams, newly washed, newly woven and true to the daily lives of the community'. Inkle and Yarico has the same magic and pertinence.

This is a narrative of deep historical insight into the commodifying and abuse of humanity and an excellent book for close study in schools and colleges. Gilroy lays the past bare as a text for the present.

Price: £8.99
ISBN: 0 948833 98 X

Gather the Faces

Marvella Payne is twenty-seven, works as a secretary for British Rail and has pledged to the congregation of the Church of the Holy Spirit that she will abstain from sex before marriage. When she repulses the groping hands of the trainee-deacon, Carlton Springle, she resigns herself to growing old with her mother, father and Bible-soaked aunts. But Aunt Julie has other ideas and finds Marvella a penfriend from her native Guyana. When good fortune allows the couple to meet, Marvella awakens to new possibilities as she realises how bound she has been by the voices of her dependent, cosseted childhood. But will marriage be another entrapment, another loss of self?

Price £7.99
ISBN 0-948833-88-2

In Praise of Love and Children

After false starts in teaching and social work, Melda Hayley finds her mission in fostering the damaged children of the first generation of black settlers in a deeply racist Britain. But though Melda finds daily uplift in her work, her inner life starts to come apart. Her brother Arnie has married a white woman and his defection from the family and the distress Melda witnesses in the children she fosters causes her own buried wounds to weep. Melda confronts the cruelties she has suffered as the 'outside child' at the hands of her stepmother. But though the past drives Melda towards breakdown, she finds strengths there too, especially in the memories of the loving, supporting women of the yards. And there is Pa who, in his new material security in the USA, discovers a gentle caring side and teaches his family to sing in praise of love and children.

Adele Newson writes in *World Literature Today*: 'Gilroy's novel hails from the tradition that celebrates community rather than the individual. Traditions are insular in spite of cultural disruptions. This is clearly marked by comparisons of culture throughout the novel. As Melda observes: "People came to the Caribbean for holidays, but we went nowhere except to family parties, excursions and funerals for ours. Talk and song were holidays to us. We believed, as the old folk had done, that it was better to be bitten by your own bedbugs than those from the beds of others." *In Praise of Love and Children* is a celebration of culture, traditions, and change. It is painful in its confrontations while liberating in its veracity to human nature.'

ISBN: 9780948833892
£8.99

All Peepal Tree titles are available from the website
www.peepaltreepress.com
with a money back guarantee, secure credit card ordering and fast delivery throughout the world at cost or less.

Peepal Tree Press is celebrated as the home of challenging and inspiring literature from the Caribbean and Black Britain. Visit www.peepaltreepress.com to read sample poems and reviews, discover new authors, established names and access a wealth of information. Subscribe to our mailing list for news of new books and events.

Contact us at:
Peepal Tree Press, 17 King's Avenue, Leeds LS6 1QS, UK
Tel: +44 (0) 113 2451703 E-mail: contact@peepaltreepress.com